ROBERT MULLAN
MOVING PICTURES

THE MAKING OF
Letters to Sofija

First published in 2013 by
Free Publishing Limited

Copyright © 2013 Free Publishing Limited

The author's rights are fully asserted. The right of
Robert Mullan to be identified as the author of this work has
been asserted by him in accordance with the Copyright, Designs
and Patents Act 1988

A CIP Catalogue of this book is available from
the British Library

ISBN: 978-1-85343-231-6

All rights reserved; no part of this publication may be reproduced,
stored in a retrieval system, or transmitted, in any form or by
any means, electronic, mechanical, photocopying, recording or
otherwise, without the prior written permission of the publisher.
Nor be circulated in any form of binding or cover other than that
in which it is published and a similar condition including this
condition being imposed on the subsequent purchaser.

Typeset in Adobe Caslon Pro 11½ pt by
www.chandlerbookdesign.co.uk

Printed in Great Britain by
Ashford Colour Press Ltd.

For Sean, Sam, Alex and Jess

*And with thanks to Odd-Geir Sæther
for the photographs*

CONTENTS

Preface		1
1.	Sometime earlier, London	3
2.	Historical inaccuracies?	14
3.	March 2012: the orchestra	17
4.	Looking for money	37
5.	March 23 2012: London	41
6.	Prep	46
7.	Returning to London	57
8.	Leaving home	66
9.	The technical recce	81
10.	Russia	87
11.	500,000 Litas required	100
12.	Some unexpected bad news	108
13.	Babushkas and bankruptcy	120
14.	The man from *The Matrix*	125
15.	Druskininkai	130
16.	Baby boys, baby girls	135
17.	June 2012	140
18.	Rain	149
19.	A Hobbit train	152
20.	Traku Voke	157
21.	To 'London' Luton Airport	163
Afterword		165

PREFACE

In *Making Movies*, Sidney Lumet's concise yet deeply informative memoir, the legendary director recalls an incident relating to the making of his World War II film, *The Hill*:

> That night at dinner, I literally burst into tears. My wife asked me what was wrong. I said I was just so tired of fighting. I'd fought for the script, for the right cast, then fought the heat of the desert, the exhaustion … [and] … now I was fighting about an idiotic ad. And that's what so much of making movies is about: fighting.

Unlike Sidney Lumet, I have written this diary from the standpoint of a novice. After a reasonably lengthy 'career' directing documentaries and writing scripts, in 2012 I shot my first feature in Lithuania, in three exotic languages -Lithuanian, Russian and Polish- with a Norwegian director of photography, a Lithuanian crew and cast, and a relatively small budget.

It has been a long struggle and, like Sidney Lumet, there have been many occasions on which I have cried, wept and experienced something akin to despair. A modest hope for this diary is that other would-be filmmakers learn from my mistakes and, through reflection, try and avoid them. And that they also learn that this truly is a many-headed enterprise: one of mystery, beauty, surprise, hard work, 'team work,' consummate skill and finally that filmmaking is an industry which attracts all number of emotional and financial predators. First, let me reminisce and dip into an early diary entry.

1

SOMETIME EARLIER, LONDON

Starbucks, Wardour Street, London. Due to the insultingly low salary level, none of the staff spoke English and ordering a cappuccino with skimmed milk was akin to asking for the mathematical equivalent of Ohm's law. It's supposed to be summer, but the day is like any other. Where have all the seasons gone? Four of us are present: me, Tony Palmer, Carola Ash and Paul Lichtmann. They are all part of the story. Tony is a veteran of filmmaking, most memorably through such music documentaries as *Farewell to Cream* and his painfully beautiful homage to Henryk Górecki's *Symphony of Sorrowful Songs*. Tony is a perennial name-dropper and so he talks about 'Richard' [Burton], 'Eric' [Clapton], and 'Ben' [Kingsley] in the same relaxed and natural way that I talk about my children. He is involved in my project as 'executive producer.' Essentially he has lent me his advice as to how my script can be made tighter and more 'political.' I have done two rewrites for his perusal and have found most of his advice to be sound and thoughtful, although I have felt annoyed when he has simply written 'bollocks' against some of my dialogue. When I say 'annoyed,' I actually mean murderous.

I have forgotten the number of times I have been offered advice on the script, but such advice has never been accompanied by hard cash. Indeed, I have changed the script many times, in varied and different ways for different producers, all of them making the right noises, but without the cash required to put such scripts into production.

Carola is Head of Co-Production at the Future Film Group (FFG) in London, a company specialising in involving themselves in film financing through tax breaks. I ask her what her specific job is at the FFG - "you tell me?" is her somewhat ambiguous and unhelpful response. Two cappuccinos later she expands: "I'm head of co-productions, but we don't have any."

Paul Lichtmann is a 'lawyer' -we think- and represents various East European film studios. As well as Lithuania, he touts the advantages of shooting in Bulgaria, Ukraine and Belarus. We talk about the weather, Starbucks, the Future Film Group and Turkey, because he's just been on holiday near Konya and was *en route* to Los Angeles, via London. I thought he might be interested in the fact that I'd made a series of documentaries for Channel 4 on *Sufism*, the mystical version of Islam, and that I'd been to Konya to research the Mevlevi, or, as they're more commonly known, the 'Whirling Dervishes.' Surprisingly -to me, at least- he was singularly disinterested and unimpressed.

Tony and I talked up *Letters to Sofija* and said that we hoped that we could do a deal with the Lithuanian Studio (LKS). At this point Mr Lichtmann, who was a plain looking yet large man, but who consistently sighed (as if he had the plight of the world on his shoulders), came to life. He leant toward us and spoke impatiently and a little aggressively, as if he was speaking to naughty children. "Okay, I've sat here and I've listened to what you've said. But let me tell you what it's all about." I was anxious that Tony might be inclined to tell him to 'fuck off.' Tony, however, remained impassive: inscrutable. Our American friend continued: "When it comes to pictures, there's only one show in town - money."

When he'd left the café, Tony and I shared our view of him. We both agreed that Mr Lichtmann had the persona of a second-hand car salesman but concluded, sadly, that indeed many of the people on the financing and producing side of the industry are exactly thus. If anyone ought to know, I should.

The history of my film is a time of joy, pain and disappointment and, in equal measures, farce and deceit. The story begins in 1996.

I first travelled to Lithuania in 1996, as a volunteer for Caritas, a charity sponsored by the Catholic Church. I was attached to the Vytautas Magnus University, in the country's second city Kaunas, where I taught psychology to social welfare students.

Kaunas is less cosmopolitan than the capital, Vilnius, and is primarily a Lithuanian-language city. It is also far more industrial than its neighbour, felt inferior to it, and the University itself was more functional than fancy. It surprised me that the University's toilets were more third than second world, an observation reinforced by my first trip to the railway station where it was almost impossible to cope with the toilet's filth and stench. Otherwise, Kaunas was a welcoming, clean and inspiring city.

My students were all women, mostly in their middle-to-late 20's. They listened through translators -actually trainee psychiatrists working to increase their paltry incomes- but they remained impassive, said nothing, asked no questions. Perhaps naïvely, this puzzled me. Why no questions? I soon discovered that these women -born, raised and educated in 'Soviet times'- had internalised the view that it was best not to get noticed, therefore would remain silent and not ask any questions.

I shared some accommodation with other 'foreigners,' one of whom -a portly and unlikeable American- encouraged me to believe that he was a member of some branch of the US intelligence service. Where he appeared to find Lithuania to be somewhat primitive, I found it romantic - in the sense of somewhat mysterious, childlike and open to all possibilities.

I became friendly with Darius, one of my translators. We talked incessantly about the social and political and cultural structures of the UK, the differences I perceived between my country and Lithuania and, regularly and increasingly, the Soviet regime in which he was raised and socialised. Early on my trip I enjoyed a meal with him and his wife, with their small baby in attendance. Their apartment was shoebox-sized, bleak and with very little colour. We listened to Rolling Stones' records he'd illegitimately sourced in Soviet times. As always, *Fool to Cry*, the track from the Stones' *Black and Blue* album, moved me to tears.

I began to visit welfare and social institutions with Darius, including hospitals, psychiatric units, institutions for the elderly, asylums, prisons and other such potentially depressingly bleak institutions. However, I decided that I wanted to learn more about the lives of these (and other) people, so with his help I began to interview a variety of victims of social and political inequalities and injustice. I interviewed alcoholics, prisoners, adopted children, gulag survivors, Lithuanian Jews and many others. I was particularly interested in how such individuals would fare in the new post-Soviet era. Personally, I presumed they'd be left behind in the free market race and that ultimately consumerism would replace state provision, social welfare and social conscience.

Among the many significant and emotionally affecting moments I experienced was when I interviewed a visibly crushed and tearful gulag survivor. On completing the taped interview I gestured that the photographer I'd hired would take his portrait. I asked the translator to explain that I wanted to "shoot him." He painfully burst into tears.

I published a book based partially on the interviews, *Voices of Pain* (Aidai, 1997), worth reading (if I may say) for the sad yet uplifting accounts of the resilience and dignity of individuals for whom the future held nothing but uncertainty and anxiety.

I experienced unseasonable weather in the late August of 1996 and the University was stubbornly cold. For any heating to kickin the temperature had to drop to a certain level for 3 consecutive days but, unfortunately, the cold spell was punctuated by mere chilly days. I was without a coat and so, to keep warm, I would walk a few hundred metres to a large museum that always felt warm, in any weathers. This was my introduction to the world of Mikalojus Konstantinas Čiurlionis.

Mikalojus Konstantinas Čiurlionis

I sat in a small room, where also stood a grand piano, and listened to gentle, relaxing, soothing music, something akin to Éric Satie or perhaps Chopin. On one such day a curator politely enquired as to whether I had also "seen the paintings?" She explained:

"M K Čiurlionis was a painter who also composed. It's his music you're listening to. You might say that he was a composer who also painted." She subsequently led me to an upstairs gallery where she showed me a series of paintings and sketches.

Day

Čiurlionis's paintings are a little difficult to describe and, without doubt, appear more unique and powerful on *repeated* viewing. He was without question a mystic, a seeker after truth, a troubled soul, a fractured mind, a passionate lover of the universe and in particular, his own small nation. All of these elements are represented in his paintings: mythical creatures emerge from trees and forests, various shapes tantalise and frighten, landscapes are carefully drawn and angels inhabit strange and unusual spaces. And all of this is painted with a selection of colours that somehow defy my personal description.

I soon discovered that this 'Lithuanian peasant' -his own words- had created over 400 paintings and sketches, two symphonic poems (*In the Forest* and *The Sea*), hundreds more compositions for piano and arrangements of traditional Lithuanian folk music, yet had died at the tender age of 35. In addition, he fought (in his heart, and in his work and writings) for Lithuanian independence from the Russian Empire, met and married political journalist Sofija Kymantaitė, fathered a daughter Danūtė who, heartbreakingly, he never met. When his daughter was born, Čiurlionis was convalescing in a sanatorium and died the day before he was due to see her for the very first time.

Much has been written about Čiurlionis's mental health and the consensus appears to be that he was, perhaps, a manic-depressive who suffered additional psychotic episodes. I couldn't possibly comment, expect to perhaps suggest that in order to create his world of visionary art and spiritual music his mind was unquestionably and invariably unique. Moreover, the struggle to be heard and to be seen, to 'succeed,' invariably took its toll.

The curator informed me that Čiurlionis's love affair and marriage to Sofija was chronicled in his many letters to her (and others, including his brothers) and collected in a book, *Laiškai Sofijai* (*Letters to Sofija*). At that precise moment I decided that I would have to write about this man, his love affair, his genius, and that it would take the form of a screenplay. It appeared to me that his story was too rich in emotion and poignancy to be a documentary. Subsequently, I found a translator and soon the letters were in my hands.

Thus began a process so painful, disheartening and cruel that perhaps only a fool or masochist would continue with it. My attempt to raise money to make this (and other) feature films led me to encounters with some of the most deceitful, pathological, egotistical and reprehensible specimens I have ever encountered. Perhaps a mere 3 examples will paint a vivid yet somewhat representative picture.

A UK based film financier asked me to double the budget of the film so that he could 'sell' the project to a German fund as a 50:50 financing plan. Naïve as I was, he had to explain that in fact the Germans would, of course, be paying for *all* of the film given the doubling of the budget. I was, albeit a little reluctantly, prepared to go along with this plan if it meant I could make my film. However, nothing actually ever happened. This, of course, is almost the number one rule of film financing: *that almost invariably nothing ever happens.* So many plans, structures and processes are hatched, various percentages worked out, extensive and detailed promises made, and yet nothing happens. I came to realise that the 'industry' consists of many people who are simply unable to say 'no I can't help you' but rather feel the need to create a fruitless yet painfully drawn out and pointless process.

The last I heard of this particular man was that he'd been substantially helped with some particular personal neurosis through equine psychotherapy (yes, talking with horses) and subsequently had become almost obsessed with it.

My next painful encounter was with a producer from one of the Benelux countries. He did put a little of his own money into the project but instead of this actually helping me, the unanticipated consequence was that it rendered me depressed for at least 2 months: almost bed-ridden. He paid for a DOP and me to travel twice to Vilnius, to talk with a small studio about costumes, actors and art direction/locations in the full knowledge that he wouldn't ultimately be able to finance the film. The DOP shared this information with me as I was flying home to London: "he does it all the time."

Finally, in between all the other people I've encountered -producers, interested parties, venture capitalists, angels, time wasters, individuals with personality disorders, et al.- I must mention the billionaire couple from America who I initially encountered after an internet trawl.

Much of my time was spent searching for potential investors. I'd look for Lithuanian 'high-net-worth' individuals, Lithuanian companies known for sponsoring the arts and other such focussed electronic searches. On one such trawl I came across a Lithuanian-born US-based billionaire's wife well known for her philanthropy and attendance of Gotham's great and good social events, so I emailed her and waited. And waited and waited. Nine months later she replied to my enquiry as to whether or not she might be interested in the film. She surprisingly -remember, by now I was largely dispirited and tended to err on the pessimistic side of life- enthused about it. She mentioned that she'd soon be in London, staying at the most expensive hotel suite in town, and suggested that we should meet.

One spring Saturday morning I met with her and her husband, who was of German-American ancestry, Jewish and actively disliked all Lithuanians (except, perhaps, his wife). To him, all Lithuanians were at heart Nazi collaborators.

It was the incredibly wealthy husband I first met in the expensive suite, apparently so disinterested in my project he all but ignored me, and simply grunted a greeting. His wife appeared, as if from a wind tunnel, with her facial features stiff and unmovable. She was brief and businesslike and curtly announced that they were due to travel to Vilnius to pick up an award - "for what?" I asked, a question she dismissed with a "oh, you know the Catholic Church, that kind of thing"- while her husband was simultaneously being rewarded by the Vilnius Jewish community for his financial kindness. "So," she continued, "let's meet there and you can show us your locations and we can talk further." I was in and out the door in a few minutes and it was agreed that she would call me again when she returned home to Manhattan to fix a schedule.

Although I found them to be a profoundly unlikeable couple, I almost skipped home and shared what I believed to be good news with my long-suffering wife, Tracy, who'd heard it all before and who'd regularly witnessed me crumbling with disappointment and disillusionment.

One week later, as promised, I received a transatlantic call. We agreed a 3-day visit, to coincide with their meetings of rabbis, cardinals and, of course, the great and the good of the small Baltic state. I suggested we met at Heathrow where they'd have to take a transfer flight, a suggestion that was quietly swiped away: "We have our own plane. We'll meet you in Vilnius, but we'll fix you up with some regular flights." Again my expectations arose, as they clearly really did have the money I'd read about. After settling on the precise details - "one of my secretaries will call you"- she ended our conversation with an observation on my evident surprise at their private plane. "Bob, some millionaires act as if they're billionaires … [pause] … we're billionaires, but act as if we're mere millionaires."

The Vilnius trip was, for me, painful. The billionaire hated being there, something he ensured we were aware of every time we encountered the local population ("fucking Nazis"). His wife was only interested in the high-end amber souvenir shops - "ship it to New York," she would tell the easily-impressed retailers- and her various meetings with the influential and well-known: "Bob, at lunch, they put me between the President and the Prime Minister."

Both of them were disinterested in all my locations, with the exception of a partly dilapidated palace whose potential purchase price Mr B sought. The moment I knew I was possibly wasting my time was when, in a taxi ride, Mrs B asked me about Čiurlionis's music. I suggested that the piano pieces were, perhaps, a little like Satie, similar to Chopin, but a lot more besides. His symphonic poems, however -and I could feel and see her yawning- were, I suggested, more like Sibelius. She told me she was friends with Prince Andrew -I concealed my Republicanism and considerable distaste for that particular freeloader- and that she was sure he'd be able to get the London Symphony Orchestra to play some Čiurlionis music. I made suitable noncommittal noises. In the taxi was my best friend, Rokas Zubovas (of whom, more later) and he whispered to me, "the woman's a fool, let's go."

I persevered for another day, listening to stories of her husband's largesse, his Wall Street success, his convoluted and extensive vitamin regime and his famous friends - Mr B: "I was talking movies with

Laurence Fishburne in the locker room and he said 'don't ever invest in movies.'" I flew home via Copenhagen, they via Italy, where she wanted to check out some kitchen tiles she'd heard about for their new London house, a request that had been met by her husband's ire, as he'd been hoping to see a baseball game. "The numbers crunch, we'll call you in a week," were her parting words.

One week later, I was with Tracy and our young son, Sam, in Fuerteventura, on a cheap holiday at a complex where the cockroaches were so huge and omnipresent that it was almost impossible to sleep. The call came: "don't wanna do it. We thought it was going to be more *Amadeus*." That was it.

Previously, I'd met Rokas Zubovas in Washington, DC. I was at the Discovery Channel in Silver Springs pitching a documentary project about prosthetics, and was staying nearby at a reasonably wealthy Lithuanian-American woman's palatial house. Late one afternoon she picked me up at Discovery and inside the car was Rokas, an intense but amiable man, at least a decade or so younger than me who was also staying with this *grande dame*. Through our subsequent and somewhat meandering conversation I discovered that Rokas was a concert pianist, and was in Washington to play a gig and indeed was the great-grandson of Čiurlionis. It was, in a sense, too good to be true, and from that moment onwards our initial relationship and evolving friendship slowly but inexorably moved the project forward.

I hesitantly gave Rokas the screenplay on that first night. Next morning he said he'd stayed up all night and that his eyes had stung with tears. "Tears?" He said that the screenplay had moved him greatly. We talked all day about Čiurlionis, the film, and then I listened to his concert. We became the best of friends and he began to refer to me as his "big brother."

2

HISTORICAL INACCURACIES?

November 2011

Since that first meeting I'd stopped, restarted, again stopped the project, found and lost financiers, and met leading actors who, unsurprisingly, lost interest when the finance never arrived and they had to get on with the rest of their lives. Then I met a well-acquainted London-based Lithuanian (note, not all exiled Lithuanians work in London cafés, East Anglian farms or in the Republic of Ireland) who suggested I considered one of Lithuania's most well-known and internationally respected concert pianists for the role of Čiurlionis. Apparently he'd spoken informally with this performer and he was, apparently, interested. I mentioned this to Rokas who was quietly and politely outraged. "Yes, he's a great pianist, but if you're going to cast a musician as Čiurlionis it should be me." Yes, of course, why didn't I think of that? Over emails we decided that we would indeed follow that path. Almost simultaneously a friend said he'd put some cash into the film. If I'd believed in God or the Gods, I'd have considered this a sign.

I travelled to Vilnius two weeks later to begin preliminary discussions with Rokas and a local producer, Kęstutis (Kestas) Drazdauskas, whom I'd known since he worked on the Warner Brothers' television series *The New Adventures of Robin Hood*. Rokas met me at the airport and was not the happy bunny I'd expected. We went for a meal -as ever, pancakes- and it quickly became apparent that he'd spotted some 'historical inaccuracies' in the script and this had led him to question whether I was up to the screenwriting task in hand. Despite growing irritation and mild anger, I pointed out that I would listen to all his observations, yet reminded him that the film was a work of fiction, not a documentary. "Besides," I added, "a film is more than the initial screenplay."

All of my pleadings appeared to be insufficient to calm his misgivings. But we were friends and agreed to continue with the project but with my attention more on historical detail and accuracy. He'd given 2 examples: he thought, contrary to my script, that Dr Basanavičius, one of the great leaders of the early twentieth century Lithuanian independence movement, never ever spoke in public. And he was also concerned that I'd included a scene depicting the Kražiai slaughter of Catholics. I told him that I'd take away the Kražiai caption which he said would be acceptable, but he obviously agreed that the Cossacks had indeed murdered many Catholics protecting their churches.

After a sleepless night I decided to get to the bottom of the Dr Basanavičius issue. I visited the Signatories' House (Signataru Narnai) where, in 1918, a group of men signed Lithuania's declaration of independence. I was the only visitor at this small but quite charming museum. Dr Basanavičius was a central figure in the independence movement and one of the rooms in the museum was a kind of reconstruction, including a stuffed kestrel-type bird, his favourite pet.

My guide was a Lithuanian history graduate, who spoke good English, thank God, and who was also forthcoming about wider issues I felt the need to discuss. She repeated something I'd regularly heard, namely that the older generation had mixed feelings about the more recent (1991) independence and, indeed, that many of this particular generation would prefer a return to the Soviet certainties of the recent past. She was aware of the complex truths behind this: many of the older generation talk of the Soviet system of guaranteed homes, education and jobs, but omit the fact that many workers were forced to relocate thousands of miles for such employment. And who could forget the substantial Lithuanian forced exodus to the Siberian gulags, the White Sea or Tajikistan?

But she confirmed that Dr Basanavičius never spoke at political meetings, keeping his thoughts and demands on paper. I made the changes on the script and next time we met Rokas offered a more relaxed smile.

The question of historical accuracies or otherwise, became quite central to the events that unfolded in the following weeks.

3

MARCH 2012: THE ORCHESTRA

The initial sum of money had generated some more, enough to start the ball rolling.

I arrived in Vilnius to prepare for a few days shooting. We'd arranged to shoot a central scene where Čiurlionis conducts a Russian orchestra in St. Petersburg, where they play his symphonic poem, *In the Forest* (*Miške*). The previous November we'd met with Ruta Prusevičienė, the truly charming Director of the National Philharmonic Society, who'd agreed to allow us to record the orchestra for the film's soundtrack and for us to film the scene with Čiurlionis and the orchestra, all free of charge. 80 musicians and a hall, for free! Rokas had arranged for the orchestra to play the Čiurlionis pieces for the soundtrack in their original form. For the uneducated ear, like mine, this essentially represented a slowing down of the more recent arrangements.

Prior to my arrival, however, I'd got into endless and increasingly sarcastic disputes with Kęstutis ('Kestas') Drazdauskas, the Lithuanian producer. He'd let me know that Russian orchestras *circa* 1908 were all male, whereas the Lithuanian orchestra we were to work with was of mixed gender. My attitude was,

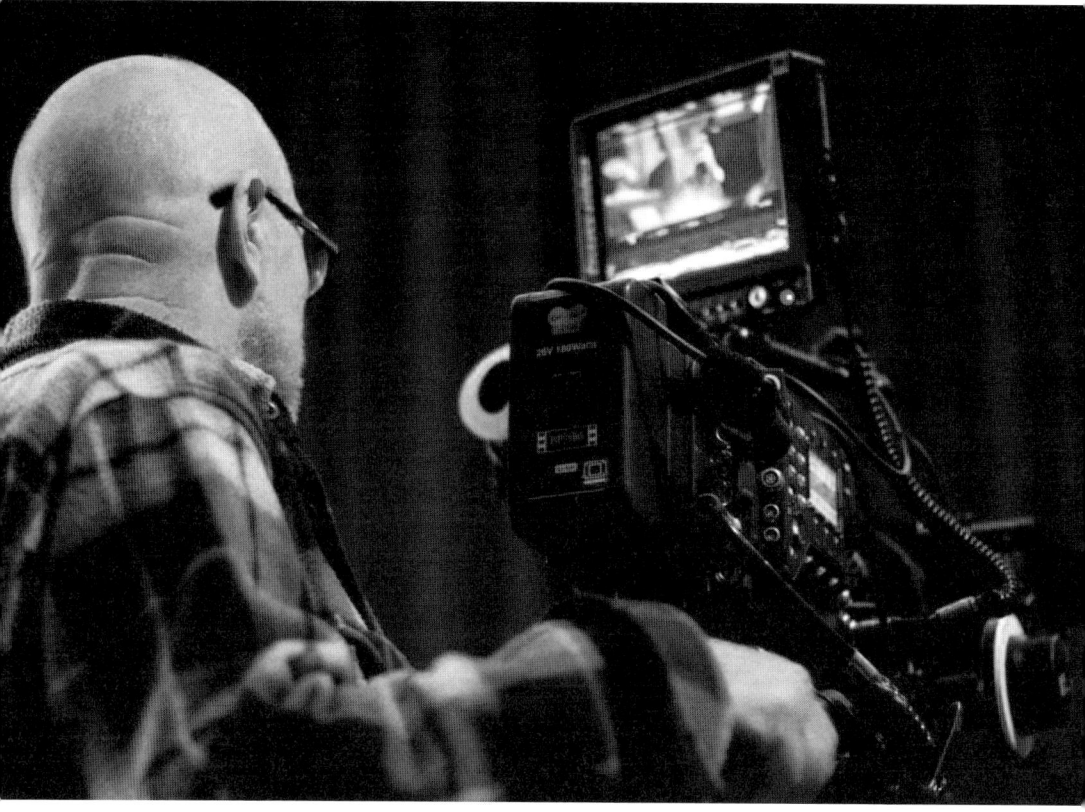

Odd-Geir Sæther

'who knows and who cares?' Does the cinemagoer in Soho's Curzon cinema know of such things? Would they care? The scene is only a few minutes long, and the orchestral membership is, in a sense, incidental to the main story, which is Čiurlionis talking to them about the origins and meaning of his composition. Emails flew between us and we were on the verge of calling the shoot off. I explained that were we not to take advantage of the opportunity, another window many never again open. In the end, Kestas and his colleagues found ways of creating a 1908 orchestra, including fully dressed and moustached musicians.

I also decided that while I had the Director of Photography (DOP) for 4 days, we'd shoot some other material: some panoramic shots of Vilnius Old Town, morning and night, and we'd use another camera (Canon SD) to shoot the candlelit mass at the Russian Orthodox Church of the Holy Mother of God (Skaisciansions Dievo Motinnos Cerkve). The DOP had earlier assured me that the Canon would deal with that particular light better than our main camera, the Arri Alexa.

Learning about digital cameras has been an education that, I suspect, I have failed. All I've ever wanted is a camera that (almost) reproduces film quality. We couldn't afford film on this project so the next best thing is the Arri Alexa, or at least, so I'm told. Once that decision had been made there followed endless discussions and a steep learning curve about capacity and storage, as well as separate issues like aspect ratios.

Throughout all of this the DOP has been patient. Odd-Geir Sæther is a 71-year-old Norwegian, best known for his cinematography on Peter Watkins' film about Edvard Munch. We first met a few years ago when I picked his rental company, Lighthouse, out of the Norwegian 'yellow pages.' I'd been commissioned by the Norwegian Broadcasting Corporation (NRK) to make a film about Axel Jensen, a one-time friend and resident of R. D. Laing's Kingsley Hall experiment, when the so-called 'sane' and the so-called 'insane' shared a living space (see my *Mad to be Normal*, for a brief discussion). Axel was terminally ill with Motor Neurone Disease. On arrival in Oslo, my friend and cameraman Laurie Yule, and I, scanned the airport for this (to us) oddly named man who was to meet us with his van of equipment. Eventually the three of us met: he was very small, wide-eyed, and wore some kind of Moroccan-style hat. We drove from Oslo to Kristiansand and on the journey we talked about prostate issues. He told us for some strange reason about various remedies for various urinary conditions – it was a quite unusual and quite bizarre experience.

Then we stayed at a converted lighthouse with, allegedly, an ex-girlfriend of Eric Clapton. While there, I encountered Odd stark naked walking around the dwelling whistling loudly.

It was only when, on the third day of the Norwegian shoot, Odd-Geir quietly made a suggestion about a shot's framing that I discovered he wasn't merely a rental man. Over the following week his brilliance shone, yet he was modest enough not to embarrass either Laurie or I. He possessed wonderful qualities: imagination, a sound technique, a sense of humour and a welcome pragmatism. Odd-Geir would react with equanimity whether we had 5 minutes or 5 hours to light a scene or interview. I decided there and then that should I ever get the finance to make a feature film he would be the first person I'd call.

I spent the rest of the day looking at costumes for the 4 actors involved in the orchestra shoot: Rokas (Čiurlionis), Inga Mikutaviciutė (Sofija), and Andrius Bialobžeskis and Agnė Sunklodaitė (Mr and Mrs Dobuzhinsky). The only speaking part was Rokas's.

March 3rd

I met with Kestas and we behaved with one another as if we'd never ever previously spoken a bad word. I saw the inside of the Hall and it seemed enormous. Many things needed altering - modern light bulbs removed, a huge organ needed to be covered by a drape, and many, many, things had simply to be avoided. However, the biggest issue, for me, was the financially expensive issue of the audience. The budget could only run to 50 extras, yet the Hall could seat well over 600. Kestas was tired, having just returned from a 3 week shoot in deathly Finnish temperatures (producing a film about Santa Claus) and was not wearing his thinking cap, so I talked with Rokas about the problem, especially as the shoot was only 5 days away.

I had a few hours free so I visited the Kaziukas Fair ('little Casimir's Fair'), an event traditionally held on the nearest Sunday to St. Casimir's Day. I discovered that St. Casimir was the patron saint of both Lithuania and Poland. All of the main streets of the Old Town and the main route to the Parliament building (Seimas) Gedimino prospectus were full of stalls, with people from all over Lithuania selling their wares – baskets, linen goods, woollen items, carved wooden statues including my favourite the somewhat sorrowful Christ figure, *Rupintojėlis* [this Christ-like figure, which comes in many sizes and shapes, shows a man -sometimes with a crown of thorns, but not always- with his head leaning on his hand and with sorrowful eyes. As if to say, "why me?" or "what can I do?"], and thousands of people enjoying the spectacle and the alcohol on sale. It was exceedingly jolly. There was also a lengthy procession, a small musical band and many people marching, some pulling logs, some on horseback, many dressed as warriors from a bygone age, and an equal number in national costume. For some reason the jollity of it all reminded me of the early scenes in *Groundhog Day* when Bill Murray first encounters all the seemingly-mindlessly-happy residents of Punxsutawney.

I had the acute sense that Lithuania was not only fiercely nationalistic but also that despite the powerful Catholic Church its pagan roots were perhaps just as strong.

In the evening Rokas informed me that the problem of the additional 550 extras was solved. "How come?" He'd spoken to a friend of a friend who'd said that if we needed 550 well-behaved extras he'd enlist the help of "the repressive forces." So, it seems that after a couple of telephone calls, we have ourselves 550 army cadets. Obviously a few wigs and a wide-angle lens and some appropriate lights will be required to conceal their uniform identity.

Another sleepless night, full of anxiety and fear and with the additional factor of a stomach disorder.

March 4th

One of the things I like about Lithuania, especially in Vilnius Old Town, is that there is a very little street litter. There is also very little noise from passing cars, and in particular no gangsta rap music repeated or mimed by scary passengers. People speak more quietly than in London and there are fewer lights, fewer advertisements. Walking through the centre of Vilnius you are more likely to hear classical music than manufactured pop. In shops, there is very little 'have a nice day' or 'you're welcome,' and indeed occasionally there is downright rudeness or disinterest. In a sense, quite refreshing, at least in the beginning.

Kestas, Rokas and I today meet with Audrius Stonys, a documentary filmmaker and the country's representative on Eurimages. We were seeking advice as to whether we should apply for some possible 17% of our budget, but it became clear we had insufficient proverbial ducks in a row. We couldn't work on a UK-Lithuanian co-production because the UK had pulled out of Eurimages, although it was now considering re-joining this EU institution. Audrius spoke of what he saw as UK arrogance: apparently the UK has asked Eurimages to give reasons why the UK should in fact rejoin. I cringed at this but it wasn't a particular surprise.

Audrius spoke of his own current project that has been shot over many months, if not years. A friend's father had, in 1944, buried a Russian and German soldier, together, under an oak tree. The son felt he had to talk about this and told Audrius who, subsequently, gained permission to dig up the bones. He now has begun the complex and challenging task of establishing identities and then tracing relatives. All he previously recovered was bones, no clothing or other items, with the exception of the Russian soldier's water bottle, still full of liquid.

20.00 hours

I've just been watching the Russian presidential election on the various TV channels, all claiming a corrupt election. Indeed Rokas told me an election joke this morning: Putin returns to the Kremlin and is told there's good and bad news. "So?" "You've won the election and you're President." "So, what's the bad news?" "No one voted for you."

On the same CNN Channel, Obama, speaking to a joint US-Israel association, says that he won't allow Iran to build a nuclear weapon. But, of course, he failed to add that Israel could have as many as it likes.

Am now going to Vilnius airport to meet Odd-Geir, due to arrive at 00:50 from Oslo, via Riga. It's cold, perhaps minus 10, and I feel sick with what psychiatrists call non-specific anxiety.

March 5th

Odd-Geir arrives at 01:00 on Monday. Rokas and I are there to meet him. He seems less wild than when I last saw him, but he remains an increasingly energetic and active man, as witnessed by his desire to go into town for a beer.

So, with hardly a soul awake, we found a bar still open. He drinks beer, Rokas green tea, me orange juice. We eat some *Kepta duona* (fried black breadsticks served with lashings of garlic and cheese). This ensures that my sleep would again be interrupted. Although no gourmet or historian, I can only assume that mainstream Lithuanian cuisine -zeppelins (*cepelinai*), dumplings, etc.- was designed for farm or manual labourers, toiling away on hardened soil for 16 hours a day.

Odd-Geir looked as if he hadn't changed at all over the past few years, his eyes still white and sharp, and his humour still intact.

After a little sleep we visit the rental house where he encountered the Arri Alexa for the first time, discussed filters and lenses, and we left believing we had a top-of-the-range camera. My only criterion was, "which of the following 2 cameras, the Alexa or Red Epic, best mimics film?" The rental house owner replied, "You know what they say? Video didn't kill film, the Alexa did." We meet Rolandas, the assistant cameraman, who appeared to know everything there was to know about this specific piece of kit.

Then there was a visit to the lighting hire people where we met Gena, the gaffer, a bald-headed-friendly-bear who, despite the temperature of minus 10, sweated on top of his head. Odd-Geir chose all manner of lamps.

Back to the office where, after lunch, I watched as Eglė Mikalauskaitė (make-up designer) worked with Rokas and his moustache. Despite my misgivings he ended up looking as if the moustache had been on his face all his life, indeed since babyhood! Agnė Rimkutė (costume) and one of her assistants tried to convince me that Rokas looked good in a particular black jacket, but the sleeves made him look like Charlie Chaplin. We found a better one, but when I asked him to behave as a conductor he could hardly move his arms. We asked the seamstress to make some alterations.

I spend a few minutes with Inga Mikutavičiutė (Sofija) who was very nervous and very young. She is not classically *beautiful*, but has an interesting and attractive face. She is innocent, perhaps like her character. However, she has one flaw, which the unforgiving camera will inevitably notice - namely, a gap between her back teeth. I've asked Rokas to have a careful and delicate conversation with her letting her know how beneficial fixing the teeth would be and the fact that I would pay for it.

The evening was spent with Odd-Geir when we discussed the shot list. Our biggest enemy will, perhaps, not be creativity but *time*. I think we know what we're doing, but you never know.

Walked home from Užupis, the self-proclaimed independent republic of Vilnius, haven for artists, hippies and the marginally mentally deranged, and not forgetting the odd alcoholic. Its Constitution contains 41 paragraphs: including the sensible and enlightened ("everyone has the right to make mistakes," "everyone has the right to hot water, heating in winter and a tiled roof," "everyone has the right to cry") as well as the somewhat bizarre ("a dog has a right to be a dog"), but finishes passionately and forcefully - "do not surrender."

I walk home in a snow blizzard. I am so cold.

March 6th

Up at 06.00 to have breakfast with Odd-Geir to shoot some GV's (general views) of Vilnius Old Town. Despite the forecast of a cold but clear day there's a blizzard. Providing we can actually *see* something this will be helpful, as it will hopefully provide me with a specific season.

Our camera assistant was a large man in his 40's, Rolandas Joneliukstis, who was both amiable and incredibly knowledgeable about the camera. We found our way to a location from which we could overlook the Old Town, but by then the snow had obliterated almost all of the landmarks I'd hoped to shoot. However, Odd-Geir found a lens that began to reveal some of the domes and golden crosses we were aiming for. Then the snow eased and then the challenge was to avoid any post-1908 architecture. We moved into the Old Town and did a tilt on the exterior of the magnificent-looking St. Casimir's Church (sv. Kazimiero Bažnyčia). Sadly, we gained the attention of a policeman outside the Turkish Embassy and were briskly and firmly encouraged to move on.

I wanted to shoot the exterior of St. Peter and Paul's Church (sv. Apaštalu Petero ir Povilo Bažnyčia) because I knew there was a parking space in front and plenty of room to work in. The snow was easing and we worked well, although by then I'd lost all sensation in my feet. I went inside the Church and was overwhelmed by its grandeur and beauty. I later learned that Giovanni Pietro Perti and Giovanni Maria Galli created the interior in the 17th century. Inside there are more than 2000 stucco mouldings representing miscellaneous religions and mythological scenes.

I asked Rolandas what he thought the chances were of shooting inside. "Let's see." We went inside and a woman said the priest was not in but she was sure it was okay to shoot, and that perhaps we could put some money in the collections box. This I did.

We spent a fruitful 30 minutes inside, doing a tilt from a ceiling fresco down to an organ, a wide shot of the main altar, and plenty of close ups of angels and other figures. Even Odd-Geir, a fellow agnostic, was impressed by both the beauty and atmosphere of the place.

After leaving the Church we looked for but failed to find a café, so moved on to the local forest, to take some more GV's. There wasn't a lot to shoot, but we spent an hour focussing on falling snowflakes and pine trees.

We said goodbye to Rolandas and headed back to the hotel so I could have a shower and resurrect my feet. We then discovered a café where Odd-Geir enjoyed chicken and livers and I ate yet another blini. *En route* to a meeting at the Philharmonic Hall, we called in at the Orthodox Church of the Holy Spirit (Staciatikia sv Dvasios Cerkve) where we are due to film tomorrow. My hunch is that we won't raise the finance to actually shoot in St. Petersburg, so I want to shoot a Orthodox mass, cover it with choral music, and caption it like 'St. Petersburg 1908.' Odd-Geir saw three elderly Russian women sitting in the corner and was desperate to shoot a still. I told him it was forbidden and that I didn't want to cause any ill will because of the forthcoming filming. "I think I'll have to kill you," was his response.

We arrived at the Philharmonic Hall and were greeted by Rokas who told us that he'd made a mistake and the actual Orthodox Church we were to shoot in was actually another one - the Church of the Holy Mother of God (Skaisciansions Dievo Motinnos Cerkve). Odd-Geir's response was simply that he "could have taken that fucking still."

The meeting was attended by Rokas, Jurga (production designer). Asta (1st AD), Urté (2nd AD), Gena (gaffer) Vytas (Kestas's brother and his partner, Violeta). We were to discuss the Thursday shoot, with 80 musicians and the potentially huge audience. There was profound confusion as to when the musicians would actually be available from - was it 7,8,9, or 10? I was hoping they'd be there from 7 and after some dressing and make-up that we'd be able to start shooting at 8. In the end Violeta agreed to telephone all the musicians to determine the precise start.

We went over all the potential shots and I left the Hall exhausted. In the evening I took Odd-Geir to a restaurant, Mano Guru, staffed by ex-drugs users (an experiment in rehabilitation), where I drunk some bread juice (*Gira*), the nearest to alcohol I'd tasted since I became teetotal in 1988.

Bed.

March 7th

Off to the Orthodox Church of the Mother of God. We carried the equipment ourselves as we were using the small Canon SD for the candlelight. It was another cold but sunny and beautiful morning.

We entered the Church and waited for Sergei, the priest to arrive. In the meantime we persuaded a woman (with headscarf) to light some candles. The idea was a close-up, thereby avoiding her non-1908 clothes. She was, however, too quick in her movements and a little reluctant to participate, so we quickly abandoned the idea.

We were then joined by the 2nd AD, Urté (a Russian speaker) and the sound recordist, Marius. I saw the priest who I knew was a non-English speaker and so asked Urté to ask him to explain the Mass - what would happen, when, where and for how long? All I'd so far discovered was the floor area into which we couldn't trespass.

The mass began and Fr Sergei was incredible: he possessed a quite beautiful voice, had a strong and charismatic face and was completely unmoved by the camera even when we were very close to him.

We spent a long time covering the same shot - his profile rising and falling, the kissing of his holy texts. We did some pull focuses from paintings and onto the priest and then finally a huge wide shot.

Marius, the sound recordist had been holding the boom over the priest but was also aware that I wanted to record the choir. The trouble was that the choir's contribution -from the balcony- was intermittent. So I decided Marius and I should go upstairs, more in hope than expectation. However, we struck lucky, and managed a spiritually uplifting 3 or 4 minutes. The choir made a huge and enormous sound yet were only 4 in number, led by a young man whose beautiful voice came from deep in his stomach.

The choir evoked a memory: my now wife Tracy and I had been in Vilnius in 1998. We decided we should marry and -so as to avoid unnecessary fuss- we thought we'd do it in Lithuania as opposed to England. We were told by someone that we would indeed be able to marry at the wonderfully and exotically sounding Palace of Weddings. I immediately envisaged a beautiful setting, a choir and all of that. Instead, the Palace was a Stalinist building of depressing concrete with no frills or colour. We had a couple of witnesses -Algirdas, a local man we'd got to know and like, and his 'friend'- and the 'ceremony' took about 50 seconds. Truly. We presented our papers that were stamped. "You are hereby married, now fuck off." Well, not quite, but something along those lines.

Anyhow, back to the film: the afternoon was spent pre-lighting, with Odd-Geir and the gaffer, Gena, speaking about specific lamps and various paraphernalia that was way beyond my basic understanding. The stage was cleared of all detritus and Jurga (production designer) and her assistants began to dress the stage. On the positive side, the wooden music stands *circa* 1908 she'd actually constructed were fabulous and immediately created a period look, but on the down side we could *not* convince her that our framing would avoid some of the theatre lights she was concerned with.

Rokas appeared in costume. He wanted to walk around the Hall and get a 'feeling' of the place. I asked him to stand on the podium -specially constructed in pine- and pretend to conduct the orchestra. The sleeves on his jacket still looked very short to me. I took him downstairs where wardrobe had brought all the costumes. After a bout of mis-communication the wardrobe mistress reluctantly agreed to take down the sleeves. I grovelled a "thank you."

We left at 18:30, with the set almost complete.

I decided to show Odd-Geir a slice of the past: we went to the Neringa Restaurant (in the hotel of the same name) which, with its Soviet (and partially Lithuanian) wall murals, hadn't changed that much over the years. We were served by an unsmiling and uptight waitress, and had the distinct impression that *she*, not us, would decide what we would eat. The food was poor, the experience fascinating and Odd-Geir believed the grappa was one of the finest he'd ever drunk.

In minus 8 we walked back to the hotel. Full of anxiety I doubt I'll sleep.

Rokas Zubovas (Mikalojus Konstantinas Čiurlionis) trying on his costume.

March 8th

Odd-Geir and I had an early breakfast at about 06:30. I gave him an orange juice, something that, he later told me, was a bad thing to do.

The crew call time was 07:00 but I was still surprised when, at exactly 07:00, we arrived at the Philharmonic Hall and already some musicians were dressed (in 1908 Russian attire), made-up, and walking around with their instruments. Gena, the gaffer, and his crew were there as was Ronaldas, the focus puller.

I found Rokas on the stage, once more "feeling the atmosphere."

I had a long shot list, but because of the almost inevitable eventuality of the musicians leaving early in the afternoon, I'd told the production co-ordinator, Vytas, that I expected to finish at 15:00. Asta, the 1st AD, said that there were so many shots that we wouldn't have the time. "Let's just get on with it and see," I suggested.

On set costumer, Renata Petuchovaitė, adds finishing touches to the orchestra's costumes

The first shot was from the balcony, overlooking the stage, establishing an 'orchestra in rehearsal.' I decided to wait for about 20 musicians to arrive (while the others remained in make-up) so I could move some chairs, group them together, and create the sense of a large orchestra by shooting *within* the group. Meantime, while I was *still waiting* and there were only a few musicians on stage, Jurga, the production designer -who had irritated me considerably over the previous few days- looked at the monitor and said "perhaps you should put them closer together?" I am easy going but this interference was too much for me. I found Vytas, production co-ordinator, and had a quiet word, and he said he'd let her know. I never saw her again.

We took the shot, with the musicians tuning. We then changed the lens and did some interesting and effective close-ups of faces, figures and instruments. In particular we found 3 exceptional faces: a man with long and wild hair who -according to Odd-Geir- resembled a well-known Norwegian artist; Algimantas, who was to act as first violinist and leader of the orchestra, possessed a distinguished, interesting and beautifully moustached face; and finally, a man Odd-Geir referred to as Liszt. He was a flautist with lank hair and a deeply cadaverous face. Indeed it did look as if he'd been exhumed. In fact, I'd met him previously with Rokas when at one of the city's markets. Normally he wears his hair in a ponytail and when he was introduced as a flautist, I'd exclaimed, "like Ian Anderson from Jethro Tull." Rokas translated and Liszt laughed (at my populist drivel). His actual name is Darius and I greatly look forward to seeing him in the cutting room, a figure from Tarkovsky or Bergman.

Odd-Geir knew what I wanted and made some smooth, slow, moves between the players, often with soft-focussed violin bows gently appearing in frame.

Before the next shot we were asked by Violeta and Vytas -production co-ordinators and romantic partners- to engage in a purely Lithuanian ritual. After the first shot it was the tradition for the director to smash a plate -on which previously Odd-Geir, Rokas and I had signed our names- on a tripod. This I duly did and was given a piece of the plate that contained part of my signature. No one knew what it meant, but it seemed to make everyone happy.

Next up were the defining set ups of the day. The moment of truth: could Rokas act? It was also the sequence -especially the opening shot- that had given me a few sleepless nights. We were positioned at the rear of the stage and we planned to shoot *through* the musicians to find Rokas as he walked among them in order to shake hands with the first violinist. They would greet one another, and the first violinist would ask if he found St. Petersburg agreeable, Rokas would ask if he'd been able to read his score, and then following a short and concise preamble he would rehearse the orchestra. We did the shot 3 or 4 times simply to change the lenses and positions. Each time Rokas was a natural, as was the exotically moustached Algimantas.

Then came the important spoken scene. Rokas (Čiurlionis) was to address the orchestra prior to rehearsal, explaining the background to and significance of his composition, *In the Forest* (*Miške*). Of course, despite his proud Lithuanian identity, Čiurlionis had to address this 'St. Petersburg orchestra' *in Russian*. I'd written the scene in the screenplay but told him he could adapt what I'd written to his own purposes, providing I agreed with what he'd say. As it materialised his two-minute address was magnificent and beautifully performed. He said that he'd been raised in the forest region of Druskininkai, that he'd always loved walking in the forest and that this was his love poem to it. He said all this with a quiet and almost tired passion -he knew that by this time in the script, Čiurlionis was exhausted and somewhat demoralised by economic and artistic frustrations- and towards the end of his monologue, paused, sighed, and implored the players to bring his love of the forest alive.

After I said "cut" many of the orchestra applauded. As did I. I told him that he was wonderful, said that we'd do it at least two more times, but only because I wanted to change the lens, not because of any aspect of his performance.

Orchestra, circa 1908

Next up was the rehearsal with Rokas conducting. In their native Lithuanian some of the musician's engaged in banter with Rokas about him being the conductor, in the knowledge that he'd never previously undertaken the role. One called out "maestro" to considerable laughter. But, again, he was natural and passionate, eyes opening and closing, hands waving with increasing abandon. The tight shot was very effective, with his love of the music etched on his face.

I'd chosen the first 4 minutes of the symphonic poem, because at 1.56 – 2.20 there is a crescendo, which then tails off into a quiet passage with flute and (I think) piccolo. This would be perfect for the transition to the next sequence, the after-concert party with champagne corks exploding.

I've always been emotionally affected by this music. Čiurlionis famously said that when he composed music he *closed* his eyes and saw pictures. *In other words, he actually composed film music.* The music is melodic, builds, and has an early crescendo. I must have asked them to perform this same 4 minutes at least 20 times, but not once did they complain and not once did I feel unmoved by the music.

By this time Violeta beckoned that I say "hello" to the British Ambassador who I'd invited to the shoot. I'd hoped he might enthuse about the project to one of those companies who'd relocated to Lithuania, like Barclays plc -to take advantage of the skilled-yet-cheap-labour-force- and who then might sponsor the film. He was not the usual public school diplomat and appeared very normal and agreeable. While we were setting up the next shot he asked me how much I wanted and conservatively I said that, "400,000 Litas would be nice"(about £100,000), and he said he'd ask around, but I suspect nothing will come of this.

It *did* amuse me when he said, "these actors can play the instruments very well." I pointed out to him that they actually *were* musicians.

We left the stage and set up on a prakticam in the audience area, and carried out some reaction shots to Rokas's earlier speech and different shots of the orchestra playing with Rokas conducting. Next we slightly changed the lighting; Rokas and the musicians put on their jackets so now we were at 'the actual concert.' We stayed off stage to shoot the musicians in their new attire, and then back on stage to shoot Rokas conducting. Using Odd-Geir's own 300mm lens the close-up was fantastic - like being in the presence of a man possessed.

We broke for lunch after I asked Asta (1st AD) to again thank the orchestra for their patience.

The catering was basic but sufficient. By this time the 50 extras we'd dressed and the additional volunteer extras were let into the hall. Also Inga (Sofija), Agnė and Andrius (Mr and Mrs Dobuzhinsky) were also dressed, made-up and enthusiastically eating. Their contribution on this day was merely to embed themselves within the extras listening to the music and admiring Čiurlionis on stage.

I took the opportunity to speak with Inga -alongside Rokas- about the delicate dental issue. On request, she opened her mouth and said there was "no gap." What it actually was was a tooth a little smaller and darker than the others. I told her I was sorry, hoped I hadn't upset her, and reassured her that I simply wanted her to be at her best for the unforgiving camera.

I'm thinking of suggesting a *little* whitening nearer the main shoot planned for May, for which we'll pay.

After lunch all that was left was to shoot the audience reaction shots. The 'repressive forces' never materialised -"why?" I asked. "Who knows?"- so we bunched about 200 people together and focused on our period extras and 3 characters. The shots were beautiful and effective especially a pull focus from Mr Dobuzhinsky to Sofija, and Inga looked suitably vulnerable. In the role she is supposed to develop from a somewhat reserved if articulate woman into a strong widow! Mmm.

David Hunt, British Ambassador to Lithuania, with Violeta Daubarienė (production co-ordinator).

Odd-Geir suggested a Sofija pov shot so we moved space from behind her and with the camera on his shoulder shot a nice sequence while the orchestra ungrudgingly played the 4-minute sequence yet again. When I said "cut" the audience applauded and got to their feet. There's no applause in the sequence nor was it shot, but nonetheless it was a nice moment.

Odd-Geir wished to take some stills so for a short while we kept the audience and musicians in place. Andrius (Mr Dobuzhinsky), whose parents were both concert pianists, called out "*Blue Danube*" and the orchestra joined in the fun and played the waltz. I admit to a moment of tearfulness.

We finished at 14.57. Everyone was surprised, but pleased. I heard later that someone suggested that my ability to keep to schedule was because I didn't rehearse the shots and this, they asserted, was a bad thing. I'm sure there will be a little rehearsing along the way, but I much prefer to talk to the actors about their characters and scenes and leave it to them and see what happens.

The evening was spent with Odd-Geir and a suitably hyper-manic Rokas and his wife, Sonata (also a concert pianist), at a small restaurant. We talked about the film, the shooting, its financing, and Rokas's abilities, and then certain geopolitical aspects of Norway and Siberia. We then parted and Odd-Geir and I visited a bar *en route* to the hotel, where he had a grappa and I a gira. Then to bed for a depressingly early 03:30 start to the airport.

4

LOOKING FOR MONEY

March 9th

Up at 03:00 and 30 minutes later in a taxi with Odd-Geir. The pre-announced turbulence over the Polish-German border reminded me of how much flying makes me anxious and fearful. I'm looking forward to seeing my family, and also once again recommencing the search for finance, so that we can shoot in May as provisionally planned.

At 'London Luton Airport' -a joke, as any British person would know, but well might impress a foreign traveller- the reality struck that my main task now was indeed to find more money.

Late in the afternoon the stills arrived from Artbox's photographer, who I'd unhesitatingly barked at on set. They were terrific, and included many of Rokas, the orchestra, the audience -including Sofija and Mr and Mrs Dobuzhinsky- as well as some of Odd-Geir, myself and various technicians. Finally, there was one of the British Ambassador with Violeta watching the shoot. This might be useful when I'm asking companies for sponsorship money.

March 10th

I awoke at 05:00 wishing I'd taken a shot over Rokas's shoulder onto the music score on his lectern. But I know we did some close-ups on his hands as well as the score so we should be covered. I hope so.

There are already a few articles in the Lithuanian press about the project. Will this help?

March 12th

Started approaching various companies, like Barclays Bank plc, to see if I can interest them in sponsorship, or even investment.

March 16th

Rokas has, it appears, been successful at finding some money, from a couple of telecom companies and also the Siauliai Bank. He's also arranged meetings with the three mayors, of Vilnius, Palanga and Druskininkai.

Kestas has not been in contact, and both Rokas and I are quietly alarmed at his silence.

20.00 hours

Rokas telephones Kestas and it's clear that something is wrong. Kestas promises Rokas that he will write to me that evening.

March 18th

Rokas asks if I've received anything from Kestas. We begin to discuss the possibility of a Plan B.

The day passes, with no contact from Kestas.

March 19th

I send a detailed email to Kestas, pointing out that he and I have *a contract* -however flimsy and self-penned- and that we have to work together or face compensation. I diplomatically and strategically also repeat my weaknesses to him and apologise for my shortcomings. I *suspect* that at the heart of this developing problem is the way in which I communicated with Jurga (production designer), a woman he has known well for a very long time.

I meet up with Kristina Sabaliauskaitė, Lithuania's most successful recent novelist and the Lithuanian daily newspaper *Rytas*'s foreign correspondent, who has been based in London for over a decade. This meeting had been suggested and orchestrated by Rokas, who believed that positive publicity from such an interview would greatly help the film.

We meet in the Soho Townhouse; a hellish venue -not suggested by me, I might add- full of smart-arse media types, a room with a deafening decibel level.

Kristina is a striking woman. A kind of Lithuanian Angelica Huston, with her stature increased by the most incredibly steep high heels. We sat and tried to talk. A quite sickly and fawning waiter, asking what kind of water we required, etc., immediately interrupted us. It was truly impossible to hear much of what she was saying. I tried my best but didn't want to appear as if I was prematurely deaf. I noticed she wasn't using any recording device or taking written notes. The gist of what she said was as follows: too many Lithuanians -especially those who control the cultural agenda- wish for Čiurlionis to remain dead, and not appear as a flesh-and-blood character in a film; that she had always been dissuaded from listing to Čiurlionis's music because of Professor Landsbergis's interpretation; that she loved my approach - namely, making the film for the global audience so as to raise the profile of Čiurlionis. She also added that she believed that Dalia Grybauskaitė, the current Lithuanian President, was more aligned to Putin and Russia than she personally cared for.

What *I* said was, approximately, that: I loved working in Lithuania; that I was utterly committed to making the film, despite the endless difficulties; that I indeed wished to make Čiurlionis into a 'flesh-and-blood' character and indeed had included scenes in the script that suggested that he was perhaps less-than-faithful to his beloved wife; that I found working with some of the Lithuanian bureaucrats Kafkaesque; and, finally, I described the opening scene of the film where over a black screen is the sound of the opening powerful bars of Čiurlionis's *The Sea* (*Jūra*), followed by a voice-over in which Čiurlionis asserts that "the sea had once come for him when he was 17 and that it might return." She said the description sent "shivers down [her] spine."

We left the hellhole, my ears popped, and I saw her incredible shoes - 'chunky sandals' I think they're called.

Still nothing from Kestas.

I'd actually met Professor Landsbergis a few years earlier at the Parliament (Seimas) where he was, at the time, the Prime Minister. He was another example of the Eastern-European-artist-leading-the revolution. He was central to the success of the Sąjūdis movement in the 1980's that ultimately led to the fall of the Soviet Union and, sadly, the death of 13 brave protesters.

His English was as good as my Lithuanian so we required a translator. He was reverential toward Čiurlionis, coy about my project and I realised I'd never receive his blessing.

Conversely, I'd once met with President Valdas Adamkus, a Chicago-based-Lithuanian-born man, who served twice as President. Seen as America's puppet in the Baltics he was, nevertheless, far more film savvy and wrote me an extremely supportive letter, which, however, didn't lead to any hard cash.

5

MARCH 23 2012: LONDON

Kristina's piece appeared in *Lietuvos Rytas*. Translated, its Lithuanian title, read as *Why Lithuania needs an English Čiurlionis*.

Rokas later told me it was "more than okay."

I'd written to Rokas and Kestas stating that I wanted to visit Vilnius from March 25th to the 30th, to finalise casting and to meet any potential investors and do some more location scouting. I'd heard nothing from Kestas, but today he emailed me and remarked positively about Kristina's piece.

I emailed back and said that I'd made some more changes to the script albeit minor, and that I'd pay for a *definitive* translation. Kestas replied stating that it'd be helpful if I could specify more clearly where Russian and Polish was spoken, and that he'd fix the translation.

I spent an hour or so making notes where the Russian officer appears and where Russian is therefore spoken, where older Lithuanian men speak Polish and so on. There is one scene where, in St. Petersburg, two seductive Russian women, Elena and Natasha, charm Čiurlionis. I immediately write down that all 3 will be speaking Russian, despite the fact that at that time such women would invariably speak French. This is merely to demonstrate the endless complexities of the project. Indeed, it dawns on me that for Lithuanian audiences I will probably have to subtitle in Lithuanian both the Polish and Russian dialogues as many of the younger generation will know of neither.

I send Kestas some more money as I'd intimated I would do in an earlier email.

I changed the title of the film from *Letters to Sofija* to *Sonata of the Stars*, because I felt that somehow potential investors might see it as a new project and would be more likely to contribute. I prefer *Sofija*, but *Sonata* -the title of one of Čiurlionis's paintings- is okay, I suppose. In fact, I think I want to change the title, but to what I'm uncertain.

In the afternoon I meet with a couple of potential investors -very congenial people- and then head off to see an old friend, Michael Elson, whom I first met many years ago at the Moving Picture Company (MPC). At the time I was hoping that MPC would provide some CGI (computer generated imagery) for me at reduced costs. In the earliest version of the film the scenes in which Čiurlionis talks about the Lithuanian myth of Kastytis (the fisherman) and Jūratė (the Queen of the mermaids) were to be created by CGI. I was going to design mermaid costumes (based on a Gustav Klimt painting I'd seen) and an underwater amber palace, and create this through 'dry for wet' work. I'd have children in the costumes prancing about and I'd use wires and we'd create an underwater wonderland. The cost was always going to be prohibitive so, over the ensuing years, the CGI element was gradually phased out. Now the scenes are voice-overed by Rokas/Čiurlionis, there is some Čiurlionis music (with a new orchestration and a mezzo soprano following the notes: all yet to be recorded) and at the same time the camera hovers over some art work of Kastytis and Jūratė, sketched by Čiurlionis for a proposed opera (that he never completed) of the same name.

I have photocopies of the sketches, but I've seen the originals - tiny and only handled with white gloves at the MKC Museum in Kaunas. What we'll do is copy the sketches to a much larger size, print them slightly off-white and work out *precisely* what to shoot.

The Kastytis and Jūratė myth concerns the origins of 'Lithuanian gold,' i.e., *amber*. According to the myth Jūratė defies Perkunas, the God of Thunder, by taking Kastytis -a lowly fisherman- underwater and then into her amber palace. As a result, Perkunas destroys the palace, and the amber floats to the shore where it is now to be found. (In fact, I believe that the only amber worth finding these days is to be found in Kaliningrad, the Russian enclave between Poland and Lithuania. But I could be wrong).

Although the CGI has disappeared, my friendship with Michael hasn't. He's been a constant source of *moral* and, on one occasion, *financial* support. He's been involved with CGI on the Harry Potter franchise as well as other huge films, yet he's *always* had the time to indulge me in my small project.

Michael has set up a meeting with "a couple of guys" who may be able to help, he thinks, tentatively - "don't get excited"- with the soundtrack deal for both *Sonata* and also *Mad to be Normal*.

He hardly knows either of them, but he knows one of them through a "werewolf cowboy movie" he's involved in and thinks he's a larger than life character who may indeed have interesting ideas.

Ru (pert) and Matt rock up -an appropriate phrase in the circumstances- to the meeting room as if on cocaine: certainly livelier than me and both with music backgrounds. I immediately warm to Ru, who possesses a gentle face. He talked about copyright, music rights, exploitation, synchronisation, units, etc., and we agreed that I'd send him some material.

Matt struck me as either a fantasist or a genuine lateral thinker. On *Sonata* he said he'd get in touch with Fox International who had a local language slate. On *Mad to be Normal* he was far more enthused. I mentioned that the film was definitely a sixties music-based film and reeled off the obligatory artists - Hendrix,

Jefferson Airplane, Buffalo Springfield, The Doors, Traffic, Van Morrison, et al. I mentioned that in the 1960's and 1970's the Pink Floyd's had conversations and actual meetings with R D Laing -the subject of the film- when the then manager Peter Jenner took Syd Barret to see Laing after he'd endured hallucinations and other mental aberrations. And I added that Peter Gabriel, Nick Cave and Van Morrison were believed to be interested in Laing's work. Ray Davies certainly is, but I suspect that *newly* penned songs about forgotten 1950's England would not fit with anti-psychiatry, LSD and madness.

Matt and Ru talked about the well-known Pink Floyd schisms and how attempts at using their music would never materialise, and that a conventional 60's soundtrack would just be financially prohibitive. Matt, however, had another idea. He announced that he had first option on some 1958-62 Rolling Stones' music -*Jumping Jack Flash, Sympathy for the Devil, Paint it Black*, et al.- and that for £5m he could use any of such 10 songs in a film. So, Matt continued, the pre-sales of such a soundtrack would pay for the film. "Result," as he slapped the table.

He then discarded Robert Carlyle (who was actually already attached to the project) and said Ewan McGregor was "better," meaning he was more liked by sales agents. "What about a non-Scotsman?" he asked. I said that actually the actor who would really like the role was Johnny Depp. Matt said he'd been thinking of the same thing and did he have my permission to "get it to Johnny?" Knowing that most of these things came to nothing, I agreed.

We discussed Hayley Atwell who all agreed was both beautiful and intelligent, and other actresses one of whom was described as beautiful "but a bit thick." "There's nothing wrong with that combination," enthused Matt.

Amidst the laughter they left for their next performance.

I talked with Michael afterwards and we both agreed that we should take the 'who knows?' approach to it all. Besides, they were immensely likeable people.

It is almost miraculous that our friendship has persisted, as I'd earlier introduced him to a man who cost his company £250, 000 and a couple of frustratingly wasted years. A start-stop-start-stop project. This man would claim to have lines of credit from exotic banks in hinterland countries, show fake pieces of paper when, all of the time, he actually had nothing. Zilch. It is a long and painful and instructive story that only fear of litigation prevents me from telling.

6

PREP

Am flying to Vilnius today and being met at the airport by either Rokas or Kestas.

The clocks have gone forward an hour and so am up at the ungodly hour of 04:45 (really 03:45). I get a minicab to 'London Luton Airport,' the London Airport not in London.

The driver, amiable enough I think, tells me he's from Kurdistan. His English is very broken and, of course, my Kurdish is non-existent. He shouts a lot, laughs, and too often for my liking looks at me (and not the road) when he emphasises a particular point. My head was spinning by the time we pulled into the airport. In a nutshell, *I think* he said the following: the Turkish government are bastards; the Turkish people are bastards; the Turkish killed thousands of people from his town - "the bastards"; that in Kurdistan all food is organic; that the temperature is 20 in the winter and 45 in the summer; that driving minicabs was a "shit job."

I said I was travelling to Lithuania. "Beautiful women there," was his only comment.

March 25th

Rokas, Kestas and I are tomorrow going to Palanga, on the Baltic coast, where we will shoot 4 important scenes. We will be seeking some support from the Mayor, and we'll also do some location scouting. It's a 4-hour drive from Vilnius and my heart sinks at the thought.

The 4 scenes are of the 'mentally disturbed' 17 year-old Čiurlionis walking into the sea and being rescued by his teacher, Prince Michal Ogiński, who owned and administered a music school of which Čiurlionis was a pupil; sitting with his father claiming he'll never again be happy; the same scene some 17 years later, again sitting with his father and repeating the claim; and finally a happy honeymoon scene with Čiurlionis and Sofija frolicking in the sand dunes and subsequently Čiurlionis running naked into the sea.

13.00

Kestas meets me and tells me he's stressed and has bronchitis. I offer to pay for him to go to the US-Baltic Clinic but he refuses.

We chat about everything and nothing: the film is not mentioned. I listen to a CD of his band, watch some *YouTube* footage of some of their performances, and discuss their concept album - *Brothers*, based on the Lithuanian Partisan movement 1944-1953.

Still no film talk.

Rokas joins us and we discuss Monday's trip to Palanga.

Then Rokas and I go to a restaurant and he confides that Kestas's staff thought I was unprofessional: that, for example, I unplugged the monitor (untrue) on March 8 which prevented them from seeing their work. I am sick to death of all this negativity. I've sent Kestas an email saying, "are you in or out, and if you're in agree to my timetable."

March 26th

Received an email from Kestas saying he's *in*.

Have breakfast then Kestas and Rokas pick me up for the trip to the coast. It's snowing.

We drive for over an hour before we change from small talk to the film: I said we need a timetable and Kestas agreed, but he said he was concerned that we'd not have enough money. I made it clear: "one week before the first day of principal photography if there's a hole in the budget I'll guarantee it." Bollocks of course, but I had to say it. We're now all on the same page and I have to ensure that we raise some more money.

Now the tension has eased we talk music, specifically bands we like: Grateful Dead, King Crimson (Kestas's favourite), Yardbirds, Hendrix, Cream, Rolling Stones, AD/DC, and so on.

We stop at Kaunas, to have a coffee with Kestas's father. He's been bereaved for a year, following the death of his second wife, Kestas's stepmother. He was wearing the kind of loose clothing someone his age (70) suffering with a prostate issue might wear, was waiting for a new bridge for his top teeth, lived in a tiny house and, overall, appeared to be enduring a sad life. I said to Kestas that his dad had a kind and gentle face. "*Was* he gentle?" I asked. Apparently he was a communist and, more significantly, an autocrat, so, "no, not always."

We left and drove on to Palanga, having lunch at the Musician's Club - I had some cold beetroot soup and then we walked on the beach. There are plenty of dunes and the Baltic horizon (like all others) looks amazing in its symmetry. I am very enthusiastic about shooting the 2 crucial scenes that involve Čiurlionis and the sea.

Off to see the Mayor. We wait outside his office with a couple of heavy-looking guys. They are, we discover, members of the Municipality's Cultural Committee.

We enter a room where the Mayor greets us. He's in his 30's, with an old-fashioned suit and with his black greasy hair combed forward. A Lithuanian flag adorns his desk and a portrait of the current President overlooks us.

Kestas pitches the project in Lithuanian; Rokas joins in, as do the others. I understand nothing. We all shake hands. Outside the depressingly small building, Kestas tells me that we have to send them specific details and they'll try and help us with hotel rooms and meals.

In the car we devise new letters to the Mayor of Vilnius, stating that the actors and technicians we'll use will bring in plenty of litas in taxes through their salaries and therefore it's another reason for him to help us. Furthermore, Kestas suggests we use the fact of my investment as proof that the mayor's initiative of establishing a Vilnius Film Centre is working (despite the fact that the two events aren't related). All politicians like being stroked. We'll see if he bites.

We return to Vilnius. I'm tired again, as is Rokas. Tomorrow I hope to do some casting.

March 27th

I awake to a memory of an event that happened last night. I was walking in Vilnius Old Town when a relatively smartly dressed woman in her 30's approached me. Her face was straight out of a Bergman film - full of anguish and pain. She held out her hand and begged for money - "food for my children." She *couldn't* have faked her face.

I went to the Signatories House to look for photographs of the Russian army in Vilnius, 1900. The curator suggested I went to the National Museum. "Is it open?" "Of course it is."

The National Museum was closed. The plaque on the door stated "we are not open on Tuesdays."

Met up with Kestas and looked at my short list of actors for some crucial roles, especially that of the Russian officer. Then I asked if I could go to Verkiai Palace (as a possible location), a 20-minute drive from the city centre. Because of the increasing likelihood that we won't be going to St. Petersburg I need to fake it. I've already shot the Russian priest, although I think I want to repeat the sequence on the Alexa. Verkiai Palace -the home of the Vilnius Botanical Museum- has rooms that look 'St. Petersburg.' Vytas's partner, Violeta, drives me there and we endure a fractured conversation about March 8. Clearly, Jurga, the production designer/art director or whatever she precisely calls herself is top dog and my name is mud. I know that Kestas is fond of Jurga but I begin to wonder whether their friendship runs deeper.

Verkiai Palace is fine. It's now a question of cost (permits, fees) and logistics.

I discover that a bookshop, Keista -in English translated as *Strange* - has a copy of my book *Voices of Pain*, which I would like. I find my way there and am met by a couple of friendly Lithuanian-speaking people. The bookshop appears to be in a condemned building and it has a sniff of *samizdat* about it.

I am reliably informed that my book is the reason that Professor Landsbergis is so against the project and me. I suspect that the 'oral histories' that he especially disliked where those of a group of women who, like him, had been active in the Sąjūdis movement, yet then (in 1997) wondered what all the struggles had actually achieved. They did not recognise or perceive the profound change they'd hoped for, instead they believed that very little real progress towards democracy and justice (and gender equality) had occurred.

I'm so glad I've found a copy, as I've none left at home: I've given them to London Lithuanians in the hope of proving my commitment to the nation.

Will meet Rokas later to thrust a letter into the hands of the Vilnius Mayor.

We spend the evening bemoaning the fact that Kestas still communicates in less than a helpful manner. We eat -at a raw food restaurant- and then go to Rokas's apartment where we write Kestas an email suggesting a plan for the Palanga shooting (at the end of April, when it still has very few tourists), a plan which has to go to the Mayor of Palanga as soon as possible, and also a reminder that he has to send the budget to the latest great white hope – a supermarket entrepreneur we're meeting on Tuesday.

I get an email at 23:30 when I'm watching Benfica and Chelsea on the hotel TV. Kestas says shooting in Palanga in April is, "not a good idea" because the sea is so cold. For fuck's sake!

I try and sleep and am almost convinced that I'm going to have a heart attack.

March 28th

Wake up with a sore head - a headache that I know will linger.

Try and call another producer I know of in Vilnius. His phone rings, but no answer. I'm going to have a late breakfast with Asta Paulauskaitė a London-based Lithuanian, currently visiting her family in Vilnius. She's a violinist and well-connected. It's a personal tragedy that I only perceive people these days in terms of whether or not they can help me get my film financed and made.

Meet up with Asta in the Hotel Neringa, the retro restaurant deliberately kept out-of-date in Soviet style. Murals of happy workers adorn the walls and, unsurprisingly, none of the waiters smile. Her son is about 18 months old and doesn't sleep much: he wakes not for food but just to scream. She offers me the use of her Vilnius apartment, a large space in a house once inhabited by many luminaries including, Aleksandr Solzhenitsyn. I feel ashamed that I feel so grateful, but I can't help it: the offer of her apartment means yet another budgetary saving.

I visit the Lietuvos Nacionalinis Muziejus, the National Museum. Today it *is* open and I go in search of photographs of Russian soldiers *circa* 1908. At the entrance are a few women who work there doing *what* I'm not sure? None speak English so they set off to find someone who does: she gets too close and her breath is truly deathly. She tells me that there are some uniforms on the second floor as well as some photographs.

The museum is lovely, inhabited only by two different sets of schoolchildren: attentive and curious 8 year-olds and noisy and surly teenagers.

The uniforms are ornate, beautiful and grand. All I can think of is the cost of making them. On a more positive note, the photograph shows them on foot, not on horses. Again I calculate that there's a saving through not having (health and safety) stunt men on set.

I'm on the staircase when a burly woman tells me, I think, that she's the ticket controller and that I need a ticket. I'm almost marched down to the front desk and I pay for my ticket as I exit the building.

The incident reminded me of John Rex, the South African born sociologist who I met on a few occasions. In fact he once drove me around Sparkbrook, Birmingham (scene of one of his seminal books, *Race, Community and Conflict*) and terrified me with his driving. He cheerfully told me that he'd, "once nearly killed all of China's emerging sociologists when I drove them around here in a minibus." When he parked his car he liked reversing into the wall: "That way I know I've arrived."

Anyway, I recall John Rex telling me that before he visited Eastern Europe in the 1970's he'd had high hopes for such nations, until he visited one such place. "Giant fucking grey buildings, trolley buses, all full of miserable looking slaves." I remember my inspirational university lecturer, Norman Dennis, noting that Karl Marx wanted the world to resemble a giant factory.

I get through to Gary Tuck, a British (with an American accent - courtesy of having an American USAF father and English mother) producer, resident in Vilnius. He laughs at my predicament, whilst also expressing sympathy: "a day doesn't pass when I don't look in the mirror and think 'what the fuck am I doing here?'" He confesses that, coincidentally, Kestas had talked with him this morning about his *own* anxieties regarding the film. He said that he thought that Kestas wanted to continue with the film but was perhaps feeling out of his depth – me being a foreign director, a different way of working, 500 extras, and a tricky and sensitive subject.

He says that with the money and deferrals I have and the deferred post-production deal I *have in place* (a 'white lie') I should be able to make the film. Gary offers to *mediate*, sit us down and act as a kind of film-marriage-counsellor. I shake his hand, avoid his somewhat over-active dog, and make my way to Artbox, where I am late for a meeting with Kestas and Agne (costume designer).

Kestas is, surprisingly, energised and friendly. Agne is not as unfriendly as I somehow expected her to be. She had gone through all the scenes and broken down costume requirements. She'd estimated that Čiurlionis (Rokas) would need 24 changes of clothes. I pointed out that I'd characterised him as a poor man. So, we settled on one daily suit, a wedding suit, two shirts and a woollen garment. Oh, and some pyjamas for when he was committed to the lunatic asylum. Sofija was given 5, and so on. Kestas reminded me that we'd need double sets of clothing for when Čiurlionis (adult) and Čiurlionis (aged 17) enter the Baltic Sea - I agreed on two sets each, so I have to ensure I only do 2 takes for each scene.

Agne calculates that there are indeed 500 extras but, with economies of scale and sharing clothes with different people, the figure might be nearer 300 items. Still, this represents many, *many* litas.

Rokas, Kestas and I discuss the schedule. We quickly and surprisingly harmoniously agree that Palanga will be at the beginning of the schedule on May 15, not the end of April. We also agree to try our best to shoot in St. Petersburg, with Rokas to approach the Lithuanian Ambassador in St. Petersburg and also his friend who works in railways administration (for free or reduced tickets). Kestas doesn't trust Russian customs officers so we plan to hire a camera there, rather than take the Vilnius Alexa. If the railways don't participate it'll mean an overnight drive: my heart sinks.

Kestas asks me whether I was happy with the shooting in the Russian Cathedral in Vilnius. I say, "yes," although in truth I would prefer to re-shoot with the Alexa. He agrees, especially as he points out that the priest had a modern hairstyle. I hate to admit that I hadn't noticed.

I do some casting, for Sofija's mother and for the two Russian temptresses - or the 'Russian hookers' as Rokas and I joke. They are tall, pretty, bright, and Lithuanian but Russian speaking. Almost at once I cast a perfect actress, Severija Janušauskaitė.

Then it is on to Sofija's mother. One of the candidates is a colleague of Rokas's, a woman with penetrating eyes, so powerful that she could certainly excel in films of a different genre. Horror? I settle for Ramunė Skardžiūnaitė, a woman with a nice smile, kind eyes and, at 49, the right age.

How do I cast? I presume all these actors can act, so I talk to them, look at their faces and then ask them if they're interested in the role.

I return to Rokas's apartment and type a letter for the sound engineer to assign the rights of the March 6-8 audio recordings to me so that I can formally search for a soundtrack deal.

Exhausted, I fall asleep while watching BBC World News about more Syrian deaths.

March 29th

One of the lighter movements of the last few days is the joke telling of both Rokas and Kestas. It appears that jokes were central to the passive rejection of the Soviet regime. One I like goes along these lines: an older man lives in the basement of a tall housing block. He needs to borrow a kettle so he can make a cup of tea. He knows there's a woman at the top of the building. He begins to climb the stairs and on the first floor he thinks, "she'll ask me what I want the kettle for and so I'll have to tell her I'm making tea and she'll expect to be invited for tea." He walks another flight of stairs: "Then she'll take tea and I'll probably have to engage in pointless conversation." He walks further up the stairs then thinks, "and if I'm not careful she'll want horrible sex and stuff like that." He gets closer and closer to the top and again thinks to himself: "Then she'll want to get married and have children and I'll become a condemned man." So he reaches to the woman's door, knocks, she opens, and he says: "Fuck you, and you can keep your kettle." This amused us for hours -and, please note that both of them are great physical and facial exponents of joke telling- and now we often interject into sentences, "keep your kettle."

08:00

Off to meet a supermarket entrepreneur. After yesterday's beautiful sunshine it is raining. In fact we are being showered with hailstones. Quite unbelievable.

Meet up with Ignas Staškevičius, a well-known and successful entrepreneur. The location is a coffee house on the main avenue, Gedimino prospectus: the coffee house is empty, but expensive-looking. Rokas greets a man who looks like a Lithuanian professional, perhaps an architect or accountant. We sit down and Kestas joins us. We provide Ignas with a gentle pitch and he appears positively *underwhelmed*. He said he'd read the script, liked it, but felt the budget was "ten times greater than it should be." We almost sat in silence.

I decided to try and make headway: I told him we wanted 500,000 Litas, that he could recoup in first position, and that I was talking with sales agents. He became a little more interested. We subsequently had a more open discussion, about his medical training, his family and his interest in the recent Steve Jobs biography, his favourite Bergman film -*The Seventh Seal*- his publishing house, and so on, and we concluded that I would send him a proposal.

Who knows?

I return to the office and continue casting. I meet a Russian-born woman (from St. Petersburg) who will be perfect as one of the temptresses, and a Lithuanian-born man with Russian parents,

Nikolaj Antonov - "call me Nick"- who, I hope, will be great as the Russian officer. I tell him that he is the anti-hero of the film in opposition to Čiurlionis. I say to him, "you have to be mean." "What, *now*?"

Another actor enters the room and looks *nothing* like his photo. I might as well tell him immediately that he's not going to be hired, but we do small talk and then he departs. All of the actors are convivial people and it must be an awful life trying to please someone like me.

I meet up with Audrius, a young man who may be the film's art director/production designer. He appears nervous. We talk, and I try to encourage him. He wants to talk to Kestas, which he does, alone, and he expresses his feeling that the "film is big" and that he'll make a decision on Monday. Fair enough.

Agne informs Kestas and I that the budget for the costume making totals something along the lines of 130,000 Litas (£35,000). There's a collective intake of breath, although Agne says that she'll contact fabric manufacturers and try and get some discounts (through various types of sponsorship).

Kestas now has a bad back to go with his bronchitis! I say goodbye and tell him I'll be back in a couple of weeks.

Rokas and I eat at the White Elephant, a cavernous student type kind of Indian café. Dark, interesting music -Hindu funk- and great food. Rokas tells me that Inga was nervous after my email which asked her whether she was *certain* the role was for her, and that she was prepared to jump on a train in Kaunas and come to Vilnius to talk to me. I was flattered and saddened by her response. Knowing me and my way of working, Rokas had reassured her that there was nothing to worry about.

I'll write to her.

We walk to the hotel, via St. Francis's Church, where I envisage the demonstrations will be held.

7

RETURNING TO LONDON

An uneventful flight home. I begin to go through the script on the plane, working out the various language changes - Lithuanian, Russian, and Polish. Not a simple project. And when it comes to the Lithuanian version, as I've suggested, I'll have to sub-title the Russian and Polish dialogue into Lithuanian, because the younger generation are unacquainted with those two languages.

April 2nd

The tooth that was hurting in Vilnius was, today, unceremoniously extracted.

April 4th

Went to Prime Focus (of more later) to view the rushes. It is nerve-wracking, and then made worse when the pictures all look grey. I'm not used to seeing rushes without any discernible colour and look forward to the grade. But, nevertheless, what I viewed was encouraging.

Meet an actor, Seb Street, with Matt and Mike (Elson). The actor is like someone on fire (or speed), but charming. I agree to send him the Laing script.

April 6th

Am going to meet Pete and Charlotte, potential colleagues, and also the actor Seb. Pete, the potential investor and colleague, wants to put money into my company, Gizmo Films, and with this investment I'll be able to continue shooting the film. They are very agreeable individuals, articulate, congenial and seemingly honest.

I leave them and head off to meet Seb. He wants to play R D Laing in *Mad to be Normal*. In an ideal world, my list of actors who I'd like to play Laing are, in descending order, Daniel Day Lewis, John Hannah, Robert Carlyle, Ewan McGregor and James Mc Avoy. Seb is unknown, English, but very enthusiastic. He surmises that the budget is about £1 million and that he thinks he could raise it. I say, casually, "knock yourself out." So let's see.

April 12th

Meet up with Ru, Seb and Michael. We discuss *Mad to be Normal* and agree that we need to engage a line producer to prepare a budget: we aim for £1m. Ru mentions that he's meeting a casting director the following week and he will try and get some letters of intent from her. We discuss 60's music again and I suggest that I should provide a list of 50 songs so that Ru can suggest some costings. Michael and I strongly argue that we should make a formal approach to the BFI.

Seb's father is terminally ill with prostate cancer so I now understand why he was more subdued than normal.

Get home and begin to think of 60's music. It is both too easy, too difficult. Should they be recognisable songs, esoteric, thematic, or what? I settle on some favourites, some of which will reflect madness and violence, others the themes of passion, love, sincerity and empathy.

Small Faces	*Whatcha Gonna Do About it/All or Nothing/You really Got a Hold on Me*
The Ronettes	*Be my Baby*
Rolling Stones	*Bitch/Around and Around/Sympathy for the Devil*
The Animals	*I put a spell on you/Boom Boom*
Humble Pie	*Natural Born Bugie*
Led Zeppelin	*Kashmir*
Bob Dylan	*Masters of War*
Tim Rose	*Morning Dew*
Jeff Beck	*You Shook Me*
Fleetwood Mac	*Shake your Moneymaker/Man of the World*
Cream	*NSU/We're Going Wrong/Politician*
John Mayall	*Hideaway*
Jimi Hendrix	*Hey Joe/Little Wing*
Jefferson Airplane	*Somebody to Love/White Rabbit*
Procul Harum	*Whiter Shade of Pale*
Byrds	*My Back Pages*
The Doors	*The End/People are Strange*
Aretha Franklin	*I Never loved a Man/Baby I Love You*
Etta James	*I'd Rather Go Blind*
Velvet Underground	*I'm Waiting for the Man/Sweet Jane*
Love	*Alone Again Or*
Traffic	*Paper Sun*
Pink Floyd	*See Emily Play*
Julie Driscoll	*Season of the Witch*
Beatles	*Helter Skelter*

The Band	*The Weight*
CSN	*Suite: Judy Blue Eyes*
BB King	*The Thrill is Gone*
Blind Faith	*Can't Find My Way Home*
Jethro Tull	*Living in the Past*
King Crimson	*In the Court of the Crimson King*
George Harrison	*My Sweet Lord*
Santana	*Black Magic Woman*
Stephen Stills	*Love the one you're with*
CSNY	*Carry On*
Van Morrison	*Into the Mystic/Moondance*
Neil Young	*Only Love can Break Your Heart*
Carol King	*It's too late*
Ten years After	*I'd Love to Change the World*
Joni Mitchell	*Case of You*
Allman Brothers	*Statesboro Blues*
Joe Cocker	*Delta Lady*

Meet up with Asta and pay her some rent for her Vilnius apartment. We have a nice quiet (overpriced) lunch in Chelsea. She casually mentions that she bought her current house from Harvey Weinstein.

I receive an email from someone tangentially involved in the film industry - not a writer, director, production designer, actor, et al. Rather, a financier. He says he can offer me advice at "*only*" (italics added) £890 per hour.

April 14th

Received some photos from Agne (by email) of some of the cast's costumes. All are impressive, especially those for the priest, Fr. Kavaliauskas. Although, I have to say, it might simply be the actor himself as he has an incredible face, like a younger version of Donald Pleasance in *Cul-de-Sac* with also a touch of Yul Brynner.

Agne then follows up with an email asking me in which scene do we first notice Sofija's pregnancy? I had, of course, forgotten all about this.

April 15th

Email from Artbox, Vilnius, asking me if I could provide a summary of the project for *Media Desk*. This I do, with difficulty, as it is -for me at least- more difficult to produce 100 words than 100 pages.

Meet up with Ru and a colleague of his, Richard, from Angry Records. Richard is in his early 40's I guess, and does indeed look the type of man it would be advisable not to tussle with. But he turns out to be helpful and congenial: we strike a deal whereby the soundtrack will be distributed to 100 digital download sites (including iTunes) and there will be the pressing of 1000 double CD's in cases, with a pouch for an informational booklet.

I will have to get writing the booklet.

April 16th

There are problems with the actors speaking Polish apparently. Inga has a scene-setting -indeed *film setting*- speech, which is lengthy and Rokas thinks this might be difficult for her.

Meet up with Anshul Doshi the 'Global COO' (Chief Operating Officer) of Prime Focus. Anshul is a Jain, and so we invariably talk about India, Jainism, Lord Mahāvīra and then, eventually, the post deal. The good news is that I *do* have a post deal, the less good news is that the grade and sound mix will take place in India. If all goes to plan I will be home for 3 weeks or so, only to depart for Mumbai. But it'll be done. Anshul tells me that the best grade I can get will be at the Mumbai facility, and he'll arrange hotel and air fares!

Anshul also tells me that a feature film -minus cast- can be shot in India, on 35mm, for between £85,000 and £100,000. I am both shocked and pleasantly surprised, as I have a project titled *An Indian Love Affair* that could be shot in its entirety in India. The story is a true one: an English priest, Verrier Elwin, travels to India to 'convert' the natives but, instead gets converted to Gandhi's cause, India herself, sexuality, and becomes a thorn in the side of the Raj.

April 19th

Email from Kestas - "we need another 1m Litas in cash." He sends, for the very first time, the budget. 'Locations' are very expensive so, for example, I suggest we film at the coast on a day trip. I can just picture it: a few cast, Odd-Geir and I, no lights and a race against time. Quite doable.

I start searching for Lithuanian sponsors. A law firm email back with an invitation to meet, so my spirits are *momentarily* lifted.

Must fix Inga's tooth.

April 20th

What a difficult project this is: it's in 3 alien (to me) languages; a large cast (including 500 extras); there's little money or no prospect of finding any more; there are complex sequences to envision and shoot; and I'm away from home.

I have to write to Mike Elson. He'd mentioned, off the cuff, that he might have some new ideas for the mermaids. So I draft a letter.

"Mike.

Instead of the CGI I have found some preliminary sketches that Čiurlionis did for his proposed opera about the fisherman and mermaids. I am using those and they will be voiced-over and also in the background will be his music sung by a mermaid (opera singer).

I attach script/and a PDF of some sketches and a painting (about which, more later).

So there are 7 fantasy sequences. The first two see Čiurlionis beginning to draw and then the camera focuses on aspects of the sketch. The remaining 5 just have the camera picking out aspects of the sketches.

I thought: take the example of page 338, top picture. What if at the end of the sequence the serpent was made to slightly move (come to life)? Similarly, what if on page 200 we open Perkūnas's mouth and he blows clouds away. Would there be someone who could do this, for nothing! For experience? You could have a credit too. These 'small' changes would take those sequences to another level.

Two final questions. First: See Scene 38. Čiurlionis and Sofija are on a lake. They step out of a boat and the angle of the lake is the same as the painting (*Paradise/Rojus*), which we dissolve to. Q. Is this simply a simple dissolve? Second: See Scene 149. There is a final sketch that Čiurlionis *did not* draw. Instead I will have to get someone to do it (in Lithuanian) in the style of Čiurlionis. It is of Sofija and Danūtė in a boat with Čiurlionis (who by this time is dead) at the waterside. The sketch then dissolves/morphs into the actual characters (live action). Q. I know who the actors are etc., so should I draw the scene, shoot it, then simply position the actors accordingly and then dissolve in the edit?

I know you are busy - but it was your mermaid suggestion that set my mind racing!

Bob."

I receive an email from someone called Artūras who is, I am told, the newly appointed production manager. He asks some questions about my forthcoming visit and the need for location scouting. I reply.

"Dear Artūras.

Thanks for your email.

First thing, I won't be arriving until 12:55 (lunchtime) on Monday at the airport.

It would be good to see the University Library and the Pushkin Museum again.

My thoughts are probably the same as Kestas's, namely that we have to try and save money so we have to use locations that are less expensive.

Trains? I liked all the photographs although I was unsure which carriage you were specifically talking about. My overall view is this: we can use *steam* and a carriage *partly hidden* against a *station building* and therefore we won't need an engine. We need to shoot a scene inside a carriage that's *moving* (when Čiurlionis discusses his sketches with another passenger); in any event, *a modern train can pull that carriage* because there is no exterior shot in that scene (although we will have to be careful with the engine noise).

I am a realist and know that we have to adapt the scenes to fit in with what's available. We will have to use our initiative. However, the University Library is a necessary location that is so important because it is at the beginning of the film and sets the overall tone.

It will be good to meet you on Monday.

Bob."

I have finalised a deal with Pete and Charlotte. They are very honest, I think, and very energetic and seemingly motivated. Pete will try and raise money for projects and Charlotte will act as producer on said projects - finding cast, crew, preparing budgets, and so on.

I realise I have to learn to work with other people and not be such an obsessive loner and maverick.

April 21st

Yet another tooth problem -a strange disturbing sensation, more than actual pain- and it is a Saturday morning when my usual dentist is closed. I wander around the High Street and find one: a charming South African man who with his bright white teeth looks like an ageing film star.

I have a gum issue, and to cut a long story short, I undergo 'root planing.' The X-ray also shows I have sinus issues, as if I didn't know.

8

LEAVING HOME

Leaving home is awful - leaving behind a loving wife and a 10-year-old son. Hopefully they'll be out to see me soon unless, of course, the budget runs out and I return home early.

I have so many challenges to face, as well as so many uncertainties. Overshadowing everything is the uncertainty about money: will we have enough?

April 23rd

I leave 'London Luton' Airport full of anxiety and, sadly, so little hope. If the entire budget was already in place I would be excited at the prospect of making my pages come alive.

The trolley dolly informs us that the flight will be 2hrs 15 minutes, which is a little shorter than usual. I hope it all goes well.

Arrive at Vilnius. There's a beautiful -and, normally, I really don't like dogs- black-Labrador-drug-sniffer at customs. Then there's Kestas, whose breath smells as if he's just eaten 50 cigarettes. He tells me, almost surprisingly *excitedly*, that we have a meeting tomorrow with the Vilnius Mayor.

Meet Audrius Dumikas (the nervous production designer), Artūras Dvinelis (who sent me the numerous pictures of 1908 trains) and Jonas Spokas, location manager. We visit 3 locations: a splendid house which is the HQ of the Literature Society. A couple of rooms might be useful. Then to the Pushkin Museum which I've visited before and know quite well. It's a wooden structure on the outskirts of the city. We're shown around by a woman who is straight out of Soviet times, accompanied by an extraordinary man - his hair standing on its end as if through electrocution. He is also gay, if somewhat concealed, a wise move in this deeply homophobic country.

Finally, we visit the Vilnius University special collections library. I've also been here previously and it is a truly magnificent room: frescos on the ceiling, table 20 metres long, 11 fabulous windows (which will, no doubt, be a nightmare to light). This is where the film starts: Sofija addresses a group of men, chastising them for allowing

Audrius Dumikas's (production designer)
plans for boating scenes at Užutrakio

Audrius Dumikas's (production designer)
plans for Chekhov play at Užutrakio

the Lithuanian language to be neglected in favour of Russian and Polish. It is at this meeting that she first meets Čiurlionis and also his nemesis (my invention), Captain Rostov.

Audrius, who takes endless stills and measurements, points to some irritating little electrical boxes on the ceiling. We briefly discuss solutions but, thankfully, it is his job to solve the problem - something I think (and pray) he likes doing.

We sit outside -it's the first day of spring and it's unseasonably warm- and discuss the politics of film making in Lithuania and also the stupidity of the Municipality in being hesitant at supporting a project that could *possibly* help put Čiurlionis and Lithuania on the world map.

Back to the office where Kestas tells me the Mayor's office have now just cancelled tomorrow's scheduled meeting.

Jonas, Audrius, Artūras and I go through the script shortlisting locations. My eyes and my head hurt.

Back to the apartment where I try and work out how the gas and hot water systems work.

I feel lost and alone - a mere *one day* away from home.

April 24th

Slept okay, although I need to buy pillows. Hot water working, but as of yet, no gas.

Meet up with Jonas, Audrius and the production manager, another Audrius - except that's not his name. After calling him Andrius then Arūnas, then Audrius, he mildly corrects me - "Artūras, *Arthur* if you like."

We travelled for about 45 minutes to Užutrakio (dvaro sadyba), one of a collection of French-designed parks in the historic region of Trakai. The interior of the large house has been recently and gloriously renovated. However, it is extensively white and somewhat uninteresting.

Outside is another story altogether. I walk with Audrius who increasingly appears less and less anxious, merely quirky. He also constantly impresses me with his artistic intelligence. For example, he's constantly looking for small ways in which to contrast Lithuanian from Russian *interiors*. Also, outside the house there's the lake where we will shoot the scene where Čiurlionis takes Sofija out on a boat and where they kiss for the very first time. He notices some stone steps leading down to the lake - "Sofija could walk down those steps to Čiurlionis who is sitting down, and it could represent her falling in love with a man from a lower class." Why didn't I think of that?

After lunch at Mano Guru, we walk to the Old Town and visit Vilniaus Paveikslų Galerija (Vilnius Picture Library) where we encountered a magnificent room straight out of St. Petersburg. There's lots of blue, gold, a giant French-made clock, etc. This will definitely work as the Artists' Building, St. Petersburg. There's also a smaller room that could work as Natasha and Elena's St. Petersburg apartment.

April 25th

Rain. A little cold.

We start the day at another fabulous down-at-heel mansion, Traku Voke, situated in the small village of the same name - somewhat like a suburb of Vilnius. An enthusiastic caretaker of the empty-but-renovated building shakes my hand: another meat eater with an iron fist. Many of the rooms are usable; especially the conservatory (orangery) which will be the place Sofija and her mother have their first lengthy conversation about her proposed marriage to Čiurlionis.

We then stop off at a gigantic roadside restaurant, which looks the shape of a Dutch barn. Audrius had heard that there might be rooms available there (for the Kymantas' house). It was eerily quiet, unused, and our host was a pony-tailed silent type. It reminded me of the hotel Jack Nicholson took care of in *The Shining* - a notion reinforced by the gigantic kitchen, in which I could imagine a young child ('Danny') running around.

At the office I do a little work on the computer and then we visit a hospital, which had a derelict (but potentially usable) ward. Unfortunately out host (the unusually titled Medical Director of Economics) was discourteous and rude. It was blindingly obvious that she didn't want us there: so why invite us?

Our next host was quite the opposite. We looked around a deserted and partially renovated Dominican Monastery. This time our host was both charming and unique. The Brother - monk- who we were waiting for turned up wearing a trendy neo-paisley shirt, flared jeans and a nice fitting jacket. He was hairless and very 2012. His handshake was the first one I'd encountered that didn't break my fingers.

The trendy brother accompanied us as Audruis took his measurements and continued to worry, as is his way.

I spend the rest of the day trying to obtain a visa for Russia, where we are due to shoot in May. This is proving to be difficult.

The agency tells me that my photos are too glossy (shiny), so I have to get 4 more. I go to a photo booth: "Where is your visa for?" "Russia," I say. "You'll need matt, then."

I return to the agency with the photos and passport, and am asked whether I am flying or taking the train to St. Petersburg. "Why?" "Because if you go by train you'll need a transit visa for Belarus." God, it gets worse.

I meet up with Rokas and, as always, am spiritually uplifted. He has a sincerity and aura -though I hate the word- that is almost saint-like, yet he's also very much a man of the world.

I return to the office and witness Artūras juggling with the schedule for St. Petersburg. Will we fly, go by train or minibus? Will all the cast be available? How much will a rental camera cost in Russia and will they be reliable? Do we need a location fixer? And so on.

I try and Skype my family from a café, as there is no Internet in the apartment. I watch Bayern Munich beat Real Madrid with an elderly married couple from the UK. They're enjoying a three-day 'Baltic break.' It wasn't long before they mentioned that there weren't many black faces in Vilnius and asked me to agree that "there were too many blacks in Britain?" It was so depressing, that I decided to skip the penalty shoot-out.

April 26th

Awoke with the World Service and the good news that José Mourinho's Real Madrid lost to Bayern Munich.

Today is a trip to Druskininkai and the Čiurlionis family house.

The four of us share the usual jokes -at the expense of the Soviet Union, the various people I've met who haven't invested in the film, and this and that- and I'm pleasantly surprised when Artūras scoffs at British democracy: "you have a non-elected Queen as Head of State - what kind of democracy is that?"

The road to Druskininkai is straight and long, and the temperature is surprisingly high, around 25 degrees.

At the Čiurlionis family house I meet Darius, who I'd previously met with Rokas. We look around and quite quickly conclude that we can film there. There's also the theoretical possibility of receiving 30,000 Litas from the Municipality for doing so. I will have to ensure that someone actually gets this money and also ask for the traffic to be diverted for the shooting period, as the noise is quite loud.

Back at the office I have lots of work to do on the script: changing Sofija's scene where she gives birth to Danūtė from a maternity hospital to her parents' house, and changing a painting from the *Creation of the World* to *Serenity*.

I visit a 24hr supermarket -actually, more a small village, than a shop- and buy a pillow and some eye drops. Tomorrow I'm meeting a UK property developer based on the Lithuanian coast and also a native lawyer, not for interesting or potentially informative creative discussions, but for possible money.

April 27th

Eye red, sore, and worrisome.

At 9 I meet James Clarke a property developer based in Klaipėda. He turns up at the Radisson Hotel in a Mercedes and is Irish. He is charming in that Irish way and appears open and honest. He has fully researched Čiurlionis and the film. He's married to a Lithuanian-Russian woman and appears committed to the country. 10,000 Litas -which he sees as a philanthropic gesture as opposed to an investment- is mine. "Oh and by the way, have all the parts been cast?" His wife, Marina, is a part-time model and dancer. I agree to see if I can find her a role as an extra, which is certainly likely.

The likeable James tells me about a couple of people I should contact.

Meet Rokas and Kestas at the office of Ausra Jerfremovienė, Head of Marketing, at the law firm, Eversheds Saladzius. We do a 3 man pitch -and very well, I might (humbly) add- and she says from the start that she's fully behind the project. She will talk to her colleagues at the firm and she also suggests that we pitch to the French Chamber of Commerce, including the nationally hated company who provided heating for the city. I agree to do so.

Back to the office and out again for a lengthy journey to Anykščiai where there's a station and a narrow gauge railway.

The town is *en route* to Panevėžys - "Panavision to foreigners," quips Artūras- and again we drive in unseasonable heat. They say half-seriously, that Panevėžys is full of Mafia types, although many of the leaders are in prison - "but someone else will take care of their work."

The railway station at Anykščiai is quite beautiful. With some sand covering the stone floor outside the entrance and with a change of place name a reasonable wide shot will establish it as Druskininkai station.

Audrius Dumikas's (production designer) plans for railway carriage scenes.

We are given a key to open the railway carriages. They were built in 1899, but the interiors were refurbished sometime in the 1960's. Audrius looks crestfallen while taking measurements. I suggest we only have to use half a carriage and be clever with the angles. Audrius is unconvinced: he shows me a photo he's taken. We all look very small in the carriage: from then on the carriage was renamed as "the Hobbit train." Hollow laughs follow. Especially from me.

We retire from the heat and into the administrator's hut. We can have a diesel train to pull the carriage through forests for 60 kilometres. I enquire about the diesel noise and they say they can put a carriage in front of ours to cut out the noise. The end of the carriage can be opened so we can shoot the receding tracks.

A drive around Anykščiai only finds one restaurant-cum-café. It is like stepping back 20 years or maybe more in time. A barmaid/waitress with a savage haircut serves us: I choose a salad and, instead, get a plate of finely cut cabbage with a tiny cube of processed cheese in the middle. Audrius refuses to take a second sip of his orange juice. The waitress is unmoved. Artūras has 'protein' -our joke about chicken, after I told them a story about when a Washington DC restaurant told me that the vegetarian option was protein (chicken)- and he leaves the rice, which looked dead. If rice can be 'dead,' this was unquestionably dead.

The drive back to Vilnius shows Audrius's hidden and surprising talent as a rally driver. We take the back roads and he drives like a maniac.

At the office we continue to plan for the St. Petersburg trip and I decide that we should take Inga if available: there are a couple of exteriors with her which would be good to attempt and besides, she and Rokas could talk and discuss various scenes.

Jonas (location scout) says he'll take me to the airport at 12:30 to pick up Odd-Geir (and his wife who is going to stay for 3 days).

So, at 01:15 Odd-Geir appears from the airport laden with luggage and wearing a Panama hat. Despite everyone's tiredness, including mine, I cannot resist asking him a couple of questions, especially about how we may be able to light an evening scene in St. Petersburg without too many lights. He says something incredibly detailed and technical about the camera's ability but it's over my head and I can't pretend I truly understand.

02:30 to bed.

April 28th
08:00

Today I will try and find one of those Internet plug-ins (dongles?), as I increasingly don't think that the Internet will be fixed in the apartment. I also want to take Odd-Geir to the visa agency.

Later I will meet Rokas to go over his voice-overs, which we will try and record on Sunday - the sound studio is booked and available, but he's anxious.

Incidentally, I'd met him late last night with his wife, Sonata. They'd been to a shindig at the Hotel Neringa, where he'd managed to talk briefly to the Vilnius Mayor, Mr Zuokas. Apparently the slight chance that we might receive some help will only materialise in July. So after the promise of money, the requests for supporting evidence (which we provided), we are left with nothing. Why did I *for a moment* believe the promise of a politician?

My mood is not improved when I see the threads following a positive article on Rokas and the film, some of which argue that he's too old to play Čiurlionis -despite the fact that Čiurlionis looked the oldest 35 year-old ever known to man or beast- that the government shouldn't "waste millions on this rubbish" and that I was a "Jewish British Director who hadn't a clue."

I take Odd-Geir to the visa agency and the unhelpful woman there says that I should come back on Monday, as they can't give me a visa: "we called Russian Embassy and they said 'no'."

What else can go wrong? My toothache returns (to join the eye ache) and Rokas wants to change some of the voice-overs.

22:05

Odd-Geir and his wife, Andrea, are out. I am in the apartment and feel under siege.

22:10

I learn that Inga can't make the St. Petersburg trip -can I?- because of her theatre commitments.

April 29th

I go with Rokas to record his voice-overs of which there are over 20. I didn't realise there were so many. They fall into three categories: telling the story of the fisherman (Kastytis) and the Queen of the mermaids (Jūratė); his emotional state of mind; and the letters he composes and sends to Sofija.

The recording studio is on the edge of town, found through a drive through a small forest.

The studio is in a house, wooden, detached, and owned by a well-known Lithuanian film director. On the veranda are rusty cans of 35mm film.

We are met by Zigitas who was, perhaps, a veritable strong and silent type. He showed us to a small room dominated by a microphone on a stand. Rokas put his papers on the lectern, which was alongside. "Should I come with you, where I can direct Rokas by a button?" I asked. "No, we all sit in here."

So, unlike, say, De Lane Lea in Soho, London, this was a basic set up. Rokas began and read well, but I could hear some kind of noise. I asked Zigitas to play back a couple of takes and I put on his headphones. The audio was magnificent and I realised that I needn't have worried.

In the evening I drunk a lot of gira, the allegedly non-alcoholic beverage made from bread. I'm slightly concerned my alcoholic days are returning.

April 30th

Go to the travel agent and the man returns my passport and simply says, with no explanation, "No Russian visa." I try two more agencies, get some more photographs, feel like crying and eventually I call a London visa agency. They claim they can help so I DHL the passport and form to London.

If successful this will be the most expensive visa *ever*.

It has taken all day and I am tired, but Audrius again shows me photographs of us in the narrow gauge railway carriage and we indeed do look -as he suggests- like giants. He wants to build a carriage and kind of rock it back and forth. I say no, and intimate that Odd-Geir and I will find a way of shooting it to render the characters 'normal' size.

Not for the first time I realise how easily everything could unravel and how easily I could just up and leave instead of facing and solving problems.

May 1st

Woken up feeling terribly homesick. What can I do?

I speak to Odd-Geir about the railway carriage and he concurs that there will be a way in which -through a combination of the selection of appropriate lenses and camera angles- we can shoot the important scene on the train. Audrius won't agree, but he'll have to lump it: the train has to be dressed for the shoot.

I realise more and more, day by day, that Artūras, the production manager, is the one person who is supporting me. Everyone else is working for the film, wonderfully well, but Artūras is making my life easier and I feel a little protected by him. This is *so* necessary as I am at the centre of everything and I feel exposed.

Today I will be choosing secondary characters on the basis of photographs Jurga, the casting director, shows me.

Odd-Geir told me that Peter Watkins, the British Director

(of *The War Game*, *Munch*, *La Commune*, et al.) he'd worked with, *loathed actors*. I think that personally, coming from a documentary background, I'm primarily interested in the photography of the project as opposed to the impact of the actors. I'm also not used to working with them - I just hope to God they do their job and not cause me too much grief. The film is an amalgam of a bedrock of a complex musical score, some interesting and at times beautiful locations, some paintings that will be shot in (hopefully) a dramatic manner, sharp and imaginative camera work, and then the actors. Dominating all of this is both the story and the performance of Rokas - a non-actor, playing his great-grand father.

I am determined to bring the locations and geography of Lithuania and specific places alive.

12:00

No choosing of actors as the casting director isn't working today.

With Jonas, the location scout, I start looking for a Church that will be location for the scene where Captain Rostov and his soldiers kill some innocent Catholics.

We travel to some villages about 50km from Vilnius. It's hot again so we stop at a small shop and buy some water. One of the women in the shop has no teeth, sunken eyes and looks over 100. They stare at us as if we are aliens.

We find churches, but none are suitable. Finally, Jonas mentions a church a mere 10km from Vilnius: it's near a railway line but we can go to the nearest station and walkie-talkie oncoming trains. It has a separate bell tower that has a small door so I can have a Russian soldier pulling out a Catholic from it as he rings the bell. It feels like a good end to the day.

Sofija (Marija Korenkaitė) and her mother (Ramunė Skardžiūnaitė)

18.15

But it isn't. Inga has difficulties with her diary again. Enough is enough. I tell Artūras I'm going to replace her.

May 2nd

I spend the day talking with a short list of actresses. I've studied their faces, highlighted those with interesting looks, compared their heights with Inga -because Agne (costume designer) is concerned about altering the dresses that are designed for Inga- and I find an enthusiastic woman. I meet her. Good looking and a strong character. I show the photograph to her to my wife in London (by email) and she says, "yes, two men would fight over *her*, but not Inga."

Inga. Who is going to tell her? She can't speak or understand much English so it's not me, thank God. Artūras suggests it's his job.

Later in the evening he calls me and tells me he's done it. She's terribly upset. So is he. So am I. It is my fault: I didn't cast her in the first place, but allowed Rokas to persuade me. He'd seen her playing Sofija Kymantaitė on stage in Kaunas and was convinced she would be perfect. I should have been more decisive in the first place.

The role now belongs to Marija Korenkaitė.

Go to bed feeling sick in the stomach, guilty, as if I'd killed someone.

9

THE TECHNICAL RECCE

Awake feeling guilty about Inga but, as the local saying goes, "what can I do?" (spoken with eyes facing upward toward the proverbial God).

We go on the technical recce (tec-rec). We are in a van with a professional driver, full of the usual suspects, but also with Odd-Geir and Gena, the gaffer.

It is largely an enjoyable -including a stay for food at an Armenian restaurant- and uneventful day. The low lights for me concern audio: the forest location in Druskininkai and the Rykantai Church (where the Russian soldiers murder the Catholics) are plagued with audio problems. So these have to be replaced and quickly.

Odd-Geir is disappointed at the need to replace the Church, as he loves it. But audio is so important. This is a seminal scene and I can't let it be spoiled by the sound of speeding cars and railway trains. However, I will be asking the extras to scream and shout at the unfolding chaos, so who knows? May be it'll work?

Cameramen often appear to underestimate the importance of audio. A bewildering, but perhaps understandable reaction, I suppose.

Odd-Geir suggests a scene with a Catholic man hiding behind a bell tower. I agree that it's great and I admit to him that I wished I'd thought of it first. He tells me that many directors won't listen to his suggestions. This is perhaps stupid, given that he's been shooting films for 53 years.

Inga calls Artūras -or 'genius' as I now affectionately call him- and says it's all okay and she accepts the decision.

We leave the Church and a barking dog follows us: Odd-Geir barks back and the poor animal looks genuinely afraid of him.

Get back at 20:30, the phone rings and it is someone in London telling me my visa is with DHL on its way back to Vilnius.

May 4th

On the road checking the locations. We begin at the Writers' Building, again, because different parts of the building belong to different authorities. So it is another piece of price negotiation: and despite the fact that Jonas is only 23, albeit extremely tall and confident, he appears quite good at this.

At the Pushkin Museum the Russian administrator is not such a pushover. We have permission to shoot the wedding reception in the building but we're unable to move any furniture - not even one stick of it. In particular I want to move the grand piano -a *Becker*, 1870, only ten ever made- but she'll have none of it. There're 2 pianos in the room, one that can be played and the *Becker*. Čiurlionis has to play one of them and having 2 in the room will look stupid. I call Rokas and he says he'll ask his friend, a piano tuner, to look at the *Becker* to see if it can be played, because the other one we *can* move.

I ask the Russian lady where the toilet is: a small Russian lady emerges to escort me there and waits outside.

The exterior of the Pushkin is acceptable, except it's supposed it be winter. We debate fake snow - paper or plastic? I ask Jonas: "what do you think of fake snow?" "It's fake." Out of the mouths of babes…

The picture gallery on Dizdjoi St. will represent a St. Petersburg interior, a ballroom. It is a wonderful room, large, with a centrepiece comprising of a beautiful and ornate 16th century French clock. Everything is perfect and very little dressing is required. The possible noise outside worries me but the scene has a string quartet constantly playing (sometimes in the background, at other times in the foreground), so it could be okay.

The Vilnius University Special Collection Library is next: a location I've loved for years. *The* shot is one in which we tilt down from a ceiling fresco onto the Chairman of the meeting who then introduces Sofija who proceeds to refuse to speak Polish, only Lithuanian - "the language of my fatherland." Odd-Geir adores the location too though worries about the 11 windows. We work out the main shot and the secondary ones. The scene sets up the whole film: Sofija talks about the destruction of the Lithuanian language, and at the meeting meets Čiurlionis and Captain Rostov, her competing beaux.

Outside the library stand a large square and a clock tower. We consider it as a plan B for the demonstration scenes and we walk up the tower to gauge its potential. I fear that Odd-Geir might suffer a heart attack such is his breathlessness: but, of course, it could equally be me. The top shot is fabulous, although it would require more extras than we can afford. We then discuss the night scenes in which Sofija stares up at the stars. Odd-Geir talks about shooting 'day for night,' using the sun for the moon. Some of the subsequent technical detail is beyond me.

The day ends at the Dominican monastery; administered by the monk we collectively called 'the bro,' on account of his cool and fashionable demeanour. It is a perfect location for the sanatorium. We work out the various shots and also decide to use a basement room as the newspaper office, *Viltis* (Hope). I spot a small room in the building that could also be used as the doctor's office: Audrius, the production designer, disagrees, but I insist. This mild confrontation is something a little alien to my nature: I find conflict difficult to manage and would prefer to concede. But not on this occasion.

May 5th

It's a Saturday and another day of the tec-rec, this time in Vilnius. We traipse around many streets which are all pretty much the same, but essential nonetheless. These shots will not be dramatic, but need to be planned in great detail. However, there's an unexpected surprise in a quiet almost hidden small entrance to a collection of small apartments. On the second floor is a roof opening with a Madonna figure beseeching us all to pray. This is a scene for when the Russians take away civilians. We knock on the door of an upstairs apartment and are invited in: we ask to see the roof. It's potentially a fabulous shot; looking over the Madonna's shoulder -once we've earlier established her from below- at the terrible Russian behaviour.

Then it's off to Jerusalem Church, the location for the wedding. There are many flights of steps down from the church and I see the central shot as one that finds the 'happy couple' (and others) as they emerge onto the steps and walk slowly down. Additionally, there will also be children running up and down. The problem we have is that it is supposed to be January 1st, winter, but there are two huge *green* trees either side of the Church. Odd-Geir shows me the shot that will include my steps shots and which also omits the trees: however, it does mean I will lose the tilt to the top of the Church.

We once again discuss fake snow (and here it's paper, not plastic). We decide to give it a go, testing it before we shoot and ultimately deciding on the actual day. It will also have to be repeated at the Pushkin Museum (scene of the wedding reception).

The final two locations are the Rasos Cemetery (where Čiurlionis is *actually* buried) and St. Francis Church, where we plan to shoot the demonstrations.

The Rasos Cemetery -very Polish- is simply too noisy, with main roads either side of the interesting looking collection of graves and gravestones. We quickly visit another one, the Bernadine, and it's just as bad. We will ask Jonas to find another one.

Finally to St. Francis's Church. This is Plan A for the two demonstrations. There's a bit of work to be done especially covering some concrete, but otherwise it is a great location. There are 3 figures, including St. Francis, painted on the exterior of the church. We'll be able to use them symbolically in terms of Catholics versus Russians. I hope.

Odd-Geir asks whether we'll have horses at the demonstration. I tell him "no" because of the expense and the lack of co-operation we've so far experienced with the police. Artūras joins in the conversation and -because he values the production value of horses on screen- says he'll budget for horses. Odd-Geir is subsequently happy.

May 6th

Day off

Evening meal at Leičiai Alinė, a Lithuanian restaurant. There's a marvellous almost surreal menu: "Beasts of the forest have been cut in slices" and, as a vegetarian, a dish amused me for "meat avoiders." Strangely, the restaurant played Peter Frampton music all evening.

Odd-Geir wanted a grappa so, *en route* to Tauro, we stopped at a nice bar-cum-café, where I heard the sound of Amy Winehouse. Felt homesick and called my wife and son in London.

May 7th

Terrible night last night -drank coffee late at 23:00- so woken up in quite a low mood. In a half-dream state I imagined Odd-Geir had suffered a heart attack. He always eats a spectacularly large but largely healthy breakfast, perhaps that's something to do with it? We go to the office and then to two more cemeteries, both of which suffer from surrounding sounds, but the first will just about suffice.

The Russian Drama Theatre is next, a possible location for the backstage party in St. Petersburg following Čiurlionis's successful debut conducting his symphonic poem, *In the Forest*. The corridor is perfect - we can set up a string quartet and it is a perfect location for the two Russian girls to begin their 'seduction.'

We decide to suggest to Odd-Geir -a suggestion he enthusiastically embraces- that he flies directly to Oslo from St. Petersburg so that he can pick up his 400mm lens (which would have cost a lot to courier to Vilnius). He'll stay there for 3 days.

The afternoon is spent with the 3 main actors: Čiurlionis (Rokas), Sofija (Marija) and Captain Rostov (Nikolaj - "Nick"). I *describe* the main scenes in which they all appear and explain what I think is happening. Odd-Geir is present but not present: his blood sugar is low and looks as if he is about to die.

Artūras translates my spiel and there's much laughter.

Nikolaj asks a really good question: "given the fact that Russian officers tended to obey a code of honour, would he be aware he was acting so dishonourably to both Sofija and Čiurlionis? I suggest that Rostov probably was playing games with Sofija /felt passionate about her/was just being "a man."

We agreed that we didn't want cardboard cutout characters and that Nikolaj should follow his instincts. I said I encouraged improvisation and experimentation.

I really enjoyed the meeting and leave Marija trying on her various hats, gloves and fabulous dresses.

One of the questions I *did* want to ask Nikolaj, but didn't, was whether or not he minded being the villain of the piece. He truly contributes to the destruction of our hero. But, there again, he is an actor and should be prepared to do almost anything. In any event, I hope he doesn't change his mind: he has the perfect face, look and range of expressions. He exudes the appropriate mixture of charm and menace.

22:00

Rokas calls and says he and Nikolaj had a really good conversation after the meeting. "He's a *real* actor," he nervously laughed.

10

RUSSIA

First of all is a trip to the Russian Drama Theatre, where we discuss what needs to be dressed which, in fact, is very little. I *do* ask the manager if there are any portraits of 18th and 19th century dramatists like Chekhov that we could put on the walls, and he agrees to search the archives. At present there are photographs of the current company, including Nikolaj.

We then go to Rykantai Church, location of the scene of the slaughter of the Catholics. While there I think of a couple more shots. I also remember the scene I've written where a mother cradles the head of her dying son. I decide to ask Jurga in casting to try and cast an actual mother and son as it might work better.

With Kestas and Rokas I partake in a conference call to Eversheds in London, linked in from their Vilnius office. We pitch the project to the London marketing people: they sound, I think, somewhat wildly *underwhelmed*. Our Vilnius conduit, a lovely woman called Ausra, has asked them for 89,000 Euros. We will have to wait and see.

We take Odd-Geir to the railway station, where Audrius again expresses his concern at the small sizes of the carriages. Odd-Geir convinces him that with our frame size we will not take in the ceiling curve and hence the passengers will look normal (as opposed to Hobbits or other such small creatures).

Go to bed profoundly anxious about money.

May 9th

Wake up worried about money, a nagging and acute worry that lasts the entire day. Kestas tells me we're running out of cash. So, on that note, I leave for the railway station for the 15-hour overnight journey to St. Petersburg.

22:40

The 3 of us -Odd-Geir, Artūrus and I – are in a 4-person berth "coupe" class carriage, sharing with a 20-year old Russian girl, Elena.

We visit the restaurant car where I have fried bread. The menu has an item called, "amateur herrings" as opposed, I presume, to the professional variety?

The train is quiet, carpeted, and feels very much like the Russia of 1986 when I first visited.

01:40 (May 10th)

Woken by a highly officious Russian border guard, poking the sleeping Odd-Geir and demanding passports. She wears large earrings and has a particularly aggressive tone. She takes away our passports.

02:40

Passports returned.

May 10th

Endured a highly restless and poor sleep: worrying about film finance all night (as well as the ferocious and unpredictable border guards).

Today we scout locations with two young women from Pandora Films, Anya and Olga.

The traffic is unbelievable - parking is free in the middle of St. Petersburg so there are cars everywhere and the result is, as far as I can see, chaos. Vehicles appear to be able to go *anywhere*.

The locations are suitably beautiful and, at times, quite wondrous, like the Sailor's (Navy) Cathedral. But, to be honest, I'm churched-out. I've seen so many in Vilnius and now so many here.

Odd-Geir is chastised for taking stills in the church (of the Icon of the Mother of God) where we are due to shoot.

The huge challenge is to create St. Petersburg Railway Station -and Čiurlionis and Sofija's arrival- from being able to only shoot at a small railway *museum*. We have no extras and only a small smoke machine. Imaginative and tight framing will be the only way to solve the problem, I think.

20:00

An over-priced restaurant sends me spiralling back into the world of film finance and my general anxieties.

23:00

Still light outside.

May 11th

Odd-Geir awakes with another intestinal disorder.

I wait for Anya and Olga. It's raining heavily and I'm depressed, or at least certainly downhearted.

*Artūras Dvinelis (producer and production manager)
in St. Petersburg, with Anya of Pandora Films*

The rain is unrelenting. We find a location for the exterior of Dobuzhinsky's house that's passable (the windows are *similar* to the Artists' Building in Vilnius where his interiors will be shot).

We return to the Naval Cathedral to try and seek official permission to shoot the exterior. While waiting for Anya to receive the permission, Odd-Geir and I go inside. It is truly spectacular. Around us are many believers, kissing icons and other symbols and portraits. They appear so devout and genuine - and perhaps desperate, hoping that this will help them in their next life, should it arrive.

Lunch is in a small café. Nothing special.

We visit another small exterior and then get caught in a major traffic jam, and sit for three hours in Olga's small car. She doesn't use deodorant, and I am unsure whether or not I like the experience.

17:00

I read an editorial in the *St. Petersburg Times* that Putin is not a legitimate President on account of the way he is dealing with passive and legal protest, namely his use of OMON riot police. The editorial adds that there will be a backlash by the people but not an 'Orange Revolution,' but a revolution Russian-style - "blood."

23:00

We visit the two locations that we will shoot late at night on Saturday. St. Petersburg is illuminated with tasteful lights.

May 12th

We travel to our first location at the dilapidated palace, which is in the middle of major and extensive renovation. It is a quite stupendous building: marble structures and ornate fireplaces, hundreds of rooms, and a view over the River Neva. The scene we're to shoot is an exterior of when Čiurlionis and Sofija first arrive in St. Petersburg and have to search for accommodation. There are three shots required, but the sun keeps popping in and out and this uncertainty delays us. Eventually we shoot and Rokas is a little wooden and holds his head too high. We have a word and it improves. Marija performs with ease.

We shoot another exterior on a bridge over a canal, with one of the spires of the Naval Cathedral behind them. It works well. It's such a pity we can't shoot inside this particular Cathedral. However, we *do* shoot two exteriors of Čiurlionis and Sofija approaching the Cathedral and, again, they work well. This time Rokas keeps his head down.

As we prepare to leave there's a wedding celebration in full swing outside the Cathedral and somehow it looks a little sad. Everyone wears poor-quality clothes and together with their pained and worn facial expressions somehow don't paint a pretty picture.

It could, of course, simply be projection on my part.

The crew we have are Sergei (camera assistant) and Makar (sound recordist), who's from Siberia and quite charming. He says he'll always live in St. Petersburg, but misses the nature and friendliness of Siberia. Sergei tells me that not everyone hates President Putin, and indeed many believe he will actually find a way to help the poor of Russia.

Next up is the difficult scene of the railway station, where Čiurlionis and Sofija are arriving in St. Petersburg for the very first time. Shooting at the railway museum with no extras and no moving train is, to say the least, tricky. But this is all we have so we just have to get on with it. I've ordered a smoke machine and a truly monosyllabic man turns up with the device. We try 3 shots against an engine and then a carriage. The smoke is uncontrollable and the windy conditions don't help. The final set up is a cliché but still works well: they emerge into shot from a cloud of smoke. We then take some general shots -through the smoke- of details of the train. Will it work? God only knows.

Heavy traffic is causing us endless problems and today is no exception. We are due at the Church to shoot the Orthodox Mass but are deeply embedded in non-moving traffic. We take the decision to jump out -without the actors- and take the metro to set up. It's obvious we'll be late for the beginning of the Mass but that doesn't matter: we'll be shooting Čiurlionis and Sofija attending the Mass as they immerse themselves in the city. I know the priest was going to have a huge head of hair as Anya had previously pointed out his photograph in the church foyer. He was also wearing spectacles in the photograph but I'd been reassured he wouldn't be wearing them for the shoot: "but can he read the *Bible* without them?" I was again reassured that he could and that he wouldn't be wearing them.

So, we turn up at the church *sans* actors who are still travelling in the van. We set up and I ask Makar to record at least 15 minutes of the choir.

Natasha (Aleksandra Metalnikova), Čiurlionis (Rokas Zubovas) and Elena (Severija Janušauskaitė) in St. Petersburg

We're ready to go and the priest emerges from behind the closed doors and, of course, he's wearing glasses - as are at least 3 of his assistants. Despite being pretty relaxed about most things in my orbit I feel like throttling Anya et al.

We shoot icons, candles, the back of the priest until I notice he wears quite old glasses, perhaps even period. Who knows? So I shoot a little of him, albeit tentatively. Čiurlionis and Sofija arrive and I put them in a place near the action, which is one of much chanting, singing and swinging of incense. I ask them to simply pay attention to the Mass, which they do. Odd-Geir frames a perfect two shot and later, a pull focus from one to the other. Rokas (Čiurlionis) looks suitably serious, almost 'spiritual.' Marija (Sofija) also looks suitably serene.

Anya is now quite anxious being around me, so she quietly tells me the older women wearing "1908 black" have arrived. These are inexpensive extras. Except they're neither old, nor in black.

We ignore them and continue to concentrate on our couple, and shoot both between them and over their shoulders.

I think we have enough and I'm reassured when I put the headphones on and hear the majestic singing of the choir, a track guaranteed to cover the scene in its entirety.

We traipse to the van and have 'lunch' at about 19:00 in the late afternoon. It's the usual mish mash of sandwiches, biscuits, juice, coffee, and chocolate. The van jerks into action and a considerable amount of coffee covers Artūras.

I take Rokas and Marija to a spot opposite the Hermitage where it fronts the Neva, and to a specific position where we can also see the Peter and Paul Fortress (Petropavlovskaya Krepost). It's beginning to rain, and I'm ill prepared and freezing. We do some uninspiring GV's of the Hermitage and the Fortress over our characters' shoulders. There's not much value through the relentless drizzle.

They're not important shots so I'm not too troubled as we return to the Lithuanian Embassy to pick up Severija and Sasha, the two actresses who play the 'temptresses' Elena and Natasha. We change Rokas's clothes and drop off Marija.

23:00

The two girls cause quite a stir at the Embassy especially with the security guards. They look facially beautiful, and in their costumes, elegant and highly decorative.

We've found 2 locations for them to escort a slightly tipsy Čiurlionis back to Natasha's apartment, after Sofija has previously left a post-concert celebration with Mrs Dobuzhinsky. One of the locations is a St. Petersburg university external corridor with some interesting lighting. We mike the three of them up, and they begin to fool around. The battery light we have is insufficient so we turn on the van's headlights. There's a small focus problem with one of the takes but visually it looks good.

Approaching midnight we walk to an interesting small canal near the Hermitage and with the wet cobbled stones and some nice lamps, it's a wonderful setting. They walk away from the camera laughing and teasing Čiurlionis and it's one of the shots of the day.

Passers-by want to be photographed with the girls and they duly oblige.

With Artūras, Rokas, Odd-Geir, Sasha and BoJanna (make-up, who has a toothache and swollen face), I sit for a drink or two afterwards. The other two have gone out into the city. I get into an argument with a slightly inebriated Rokas, who claims Lithuania is free of corruption. I suggest that the differences between Lithuania and Russia aren't as great as he suggests, especially given the fact that many of the current Lithuanian politicians and administrators are the very same people (usually men) who ran the country when it was part of the Soviet Union. A proud and patriotic Rokas almost punches me in the face, but I know he's only half-joking. I leave suggesting that both countries share impenetrable bureaucracies and have too close ties between business and politics.

Go to bed with self-doubt about the shooting.

May 13th

Breakfast is a cuddle with Rokas as we forgive each other for our mutual truculence.

First we are going to the Church (Cathedral) of Our Saviour on Spilled Blood, perhaps with the Hermitage *the* symbol of St. Petersburg. Makar tells me that in 'Soviet times' it was not the centre of Russian Orthodox Christianity, rather it operated as a vegetable market. We shoot some GV's without any actors. It's a wonderful construction of the imagination and the shots really can't fail.

We try to get to the proposed top shot from the Isaakiy Cathedral quickly, but today there's a marathon taking place and so the traffic again snarls up. When we get there, in light rain, I decide to abandon the idea: how in God's name in this city of cars will a top shot find us in 1908? The domes and spires are so visible from the ground that they will have to suffice.

At the Lithuanian Embassy we pick up Marija and Rokas and do a quick exterior (of the Dobuzhinsky residence) which is supposed to 'match' the interiors that will be shot at the Writers' Building in Vilnius. The windows more or less are the same. It's a simple set of shots.

I've asked Anya and Olga to find me some dilapidated buildings but, so far, none have come up to scratch. I decide on something different to use with a Sofija voice-over where she talks about the sad and broken people of the city. I ask Anya and Olga where the nearest cemetery was located, and whether our van driver -a particularly sad and morose man- would sit for a shot. He's game and so we're off to the cemetery. It is terrific, lots of distorted crosses and in general a location with an agreeable asymmetrical look.

I sit the driver -a Georgian whose name escapes me- on a small wall and we take a very tight shot of his face. He looks fabulous; and when we ask him to slightly move to the left he does so. I then sit Rokas and Marija on a wall, in front of an interesting set of crosses. They act as if in love, him leaning his head on her shoulder. I then get them miked up and set them off on a long walk toward the camera. It's a really effective shot, and they occasionally sway from side-to-side. They talk. Afterwards I ask them what they discussed. Rokas: "I pointed to many 19th century German graves and said that I'd lived in Leipzig for a short period of time...[which Čiurlionis actually did]." He's such a clever man.

The Pretropavlovsk Fortress is another St. Petersburg landmark. Behind the main grounds is a small walled cobbled path, perfect for the walk Rokas (Čiurlionis) takes the 'morning after' he's met the Russian women, Elena and Natasha.

He walks too slowly: stops: walks: stops: walks: sighs: rests his head on the wall. All of it simply too much *overacting*. I gently suggest he stops less, and just walks straightforwardly. I want him to find his own confidence and style, and don't want to suggest too much to him. However, after more of this overacting I suggest he simply walks along and past the camera. It's good, so I ask Makar to record his footsteps on the cobbled stones and after the next take we're finished.

Rokas is quite tired. Almost emotional. "Were you thinking about how you'd feel if you'd cheated on Sonata [his wife]?" No he wasn't. He was thinking about the fact that Sonata's father was having his leg amputated at 07:00 the following morning. I'll learn to keep my mouth shut next time.

We re-shoot Čiurlionis and Sofija in front of the Hermitage and the Fortress, take some water shots (eventually putting the river out of focus), and then send the actors back to the Embassy in a taxi. Odd-Geir and I (and the Russian crew) go back to the cemetery as I tell him I feel I need more crosses and shots of 'context.' We do some nice work and finally return to the front of the Hermitage and try some GV's. They will undoubtedly need some work in post.

We finish, take a convivial crew shot (half-heartedly, with me still irritated about the priest's spectacles), and then go back to base. I join Rokas in a bar to see the last 10 minutes of Manchester City versus Queens Park Rangers, then go to eat with Odd-Geir.

A good'ish day.

May 14th

Bad night, but up at 07:00 to get to the airport. There's Rokas, Artūras, BoJanna, Severija and Sasha -Marija's gone to Dresden for a performance, Odd-Geir to Oslo to pick up some equipment- and they're great company. Rokas amuses us all with 'Soviet times' jokes, especially about the Kafkaesque bureaucracy of the time.

The airline is from somewhere in Kazan. But it's clean, seems new ("repainted," says Rokas), and they give us some food (inedible) for the 60 minute flight. The landing is bumpy -no finesse- and my fear of flying returns.

At the office I learn from Eversheds that they're still waiting for the photos of costumes from Kestas so I take control and get them sent.

Agne (costume designer) tells me that the military uniforms have arrived from Poland but that they're WW2!

18:00 hours

Audrius asks if I'd go to the cemetery, as he needs to know what to prepare. Tired as I am I agree, and once there I again realise that there's too much noise from the surrounding roads.

May 15th

I google Vilnius cemeteries and find one just a little away from the centre of town, in fact quite near the British Embassy. The Antakalnis cemetery is 'home' to the first President of post-Soviet Lithuania, Algirdas Brazauskas. Additionally there are graves for both Soviet and Polish soldiers as well as a section for artists of various kinds - ballet dancers, composers, sculptures, directors, actors and so on. The cemetery is extremely wooded with a wide variety of trees and also a wide range of both minimalist and elaborate symbols. I still favour the simple wooden tributes including those depicting Rūpintojėlis (Man of Sorrow), although there are also some interesting sculptures.

I tell Audrius (art director) about my find and we go together to pick a suitable spot. He knows the cemetery well and his favourite grave is a circular stone the middle of which is adorned with a recently planted apple tree. I like Audrius more and more: he has a haunted face with incredible red rings around his eyeballs. But he possesses a sharp intelligence, is highly talented and has a dry wit. I ask him about British music and he tells me he likes New Order and the Artic Monkeys (Prime Minister Gordon Brown's favourite band. Duh!)

We find an appropriate spot where by his graveside the priest can talk about Čiurlionis and where we can light 100 candles for a nighttime vigil.

This latter scene evolved after I saw a picture of the Rasos Cemetery (where Čiurlionis is *actually* buried) on All Souls Day, where hundreds of candles were lit. I think it will look good.

Back at the office Jurga (casting) asks me what kind of baby Danūtė should be. I tell her and Artūras that the birth scene will be bloodless, and that we will see Danūtė in her mother's arms post-birth. I suggest we shoot Marija very tight with a baby in a hospital, rather than have the baby on location: that way the baby will probably be younger.

I realise that the film's finances are almost at a critical stage. I speak openly with Artūras who tells me that we can last *a week*. I have to urgently raise money or the film will collapse. All I'll have is some footage, voice-overs and lots of dresses and props - all to be taken home on WizzAir.

I prepare a PowerPoint for tomorrow's presentation to the French Chamber of Commerce. A lot rests on it and I put in lots of pictures and artwork from Audrius.

I feel I have a cold coming on but it might just be psychological.

11

500,000 LITAS REQUIRED

Feel like a zombie today. It's clear that we only have enough money for one week's filming and somehow have to find about 500,000 Litas immediately.

Jurga and Egle (make up) bring in someone -an actor I presume- to see me. He's supposed to be the young (17 years old) Čiurlionis. He actually looks like a six-foot tall young man with a moustache. Very odd. I say "no" firmly, but sympathetically and somewhat sadly.

I am wracked with guilt over this disappointed young man.

Talk with Artūras about the financial situation. Kestas is off to Cannes tomorrow for two weeks so he clearly doesn't give a fuck.

I now have to pitch to the French Chamber of Commerce.

The venue is La Meridian Hotel, some 20km out of town. Our conduit, Ausra from Eversheds, is unable to attend so the secretary to the Chamber, Zivile, greets us. The hotel itself is a 5 star seemingly desolate place with a golf course. "We," are Rokas, Artūras and I.

First of all we listened to presentations (all PowerPoint presentations) by new members, including an American bore who lectured us on unemployment statistics and described in excruciating detail how employers can benefit from this; a law firm who mentioned, *without irony*, that one of their clients was the Ministry of Justice, Belarus; and finally was the lengthy presentation by the general manager of the Hotel, a particularly unlikeable Spaniard who spoke, French and English who mercilessly bragged about the Hotel and showed at least ten photos of its golf course.

I told them I needed money. I showed them a PowerPoint set of cast photographs and the art director's sketches, and finally described the budget shortfall.

After the usual polite applause the head honcho, a tanned handsome man, Philippe Berthaud, thanked me for my passion. We then all retired for wine and snacks next door. Philippe gave me his card and said he'd help and would email me tomorrow. We'll see. The journey home was in a thunderstorm.

May 17th

My day starts off with me worrying about money. I have a long conversation with Artūras about Kestas and we both conclude that he doesn't give a fuck.

I decide to write to him inviting him to leave the project.

I then send some emails, dodge the rain, and then Artūras and I discuss money. We need some actual cash to carry on: I decide to get some money transferred from the UK. A small amount, but nevertheless something to ensure we carry on for another week.

I meet James Clarke who'd agreed to invest (and whose wife is an extra in the film). He gives me 10,000 Litas and I give 7,500 of this to Artūras to pay the extras in cash for the following Saturday. This will result in a saving of 2000 Litas because of the avoidance of Lithuanian value added tax.

I write to Kestas.

Artūras and I pick up Odd-Geir from the airport. He brings his huge 400mm lens and also a contraption he's personally made for his Canon 5 that he wants to use while riding one of the horses at the demonstration.

I ask Artūras whether *everyone* knows the national hymn the protesters are supposed to sing: "who knows?"

I eventually got to bed praying for sleep. Tomorrow I am going to Kaunas to shoot some of Čiurlionis's paintings and sketches.

May 18th

Up at 6 to travel to Kaunas to film Čiurlionis paintings and the sketches we've had copied (by hand). The new camera assistant/focus puller is with us, Linus, a wiry energetic man of, I learn later, 39. He smokes so I know Odd-Geir will disapprove.

The Museum is as serene and beautiful as ever. Vaiva, the assistant curator, shows us into the main gallery and we quickly and efficiently start to work. I suggest some moves on various pictures and some others are static shots. We are, of course, greatly restricted by our 2:35.1 (widescreen) aspect ratio.

A couple of the sketches have to be torn or at least crumpled up, because Captain Rostov has earlier (in the script) torn them off Čiurlionis's wall. Odd-Geir lights them in a particular way in order to accentuate the creases.

We eventually leave the Museum and *en route* stop at a bizarre Lithuanian restaurant where one of the specialities is that of soup poured inside a circular loaf.

The afternoon is spent worrying about money. I meet the entrepreneur, Ignas, once more. He talks about his return, potential profit share, the mechanics of distribution and sales, and I could cry. He's going to let me know. Yeah, sure.

I take a short walk to Pranciškonų Bažnyčia Church Square with Odd-Geir to look at our location for the important demonstration scenes we're scheduled to shoot tomorrow. My heart's not in it: how can I think about shots when the money is almost gone?

May 19th

A long day -11:00-23:00- of shooting ahead of me, starting with a small scene where Čiurlionis waits for Sofija outside her place of work, *Viltis*, a newspaper office. *Viltis* is the Lithuanian word for *hope* - a little ironic given my current situation.

Odd-Geir wants to shoot the newspaper office from a considerable distance to catch some interesting light through an archway and gates. We have 4 extras, and I choose the one with the most interesting face to start the sequence. The trouble is he does look like an old crazed man. And he walks too slowly. My first mistake of the day.

The dialogue with Čiurlionis and Sofija -"what are you doing here?" she says- goes well, but I'm happier when we change lens and I can see their faces closer and their mouths actually moving!

Off to the Square where we are filming two demonstrations. Audrius and his team have built a beautiful platform where the speakers will pontificate. The extras are already dressed and ready. Horses standby and there is a motley group of extras dressed as 'fearsome Russian soldiers,' except they look as they couldn't frighten *anyone*.

The first demonstration has about 80 extras, some Lithuanian flags and three speakers on the podium. The unnamed orator is played by Gediminas Storpirštis. He has a strong and interesting face. I speak with him and reinforce my mantra: don't change the meaning but feel free to speak the text in your own way and add what you like. He says, "Yes I know." I ask him whether it's difficult to say the text about Lithuanian independence and he replies that 2012 is like 1908, and nothing has really changed. He fears that Lithuanian *identity* is being eroded (by EU membership and relentless consumerism) and that what I wrote about 1908 is absolutely applicable today.

I start off by getting the extras to sing the National Hymn and wave their flags. They do this with vigour. It looks good. Then Gediminas gets to his feet and delivers his/my speech. I'm looking at it on the monitor and it is incredibly powerful, as if he actually means it. The crowd clap and shout in agreement and conclude with a slow furious chant of "Lietuva, Lietuva, Lietuva." In between changing angles, I say to him "it seemed as if you meant it." "I do." It is reassuring to know that I've not got everything wrong, a feeling I sadly but regularly experience.

The second angle is across his face and up to a picture of St. Francis high on the Church. It works well, and then we follow it up with a shot from behind him to the crowd and picking out Rokas (Čiurlionis). It's now time for the first horses and soldiers' sequences, where Nikolaj (Captain Rostov) orders his men to rough up the crowd. He will shout the order and there will be 4 rounds of fire, then the soldiers will move in.

Nikolaj is seated on a horse with appropriately, a stern facial expression. On cue the 4 shots are fired and his horse (a 'stunt horse') goes berserk and all but throws him to the floor. We try it a couple of more times and then abandon it up for this particular demonstration. He shouts the order standing and as the soldiers move to the crowd Odd-Geir keeps the camera on him as he menacingly approaches the crowd. It's a chilling and wonderful shot. The crowd gets a little roughed up and we break for some food.

The extras -dressed in clothes ranging from peasants to the wealthy of all ages, shapes and sizes- are tired from singing and avoiding bayonets.

For the second demonstration (which occurs some 50 pages later in the script) where Sofija speaks, I've ordered a cherry picker. Odd-Geir approved of the idea and has a position high up against the church wall where the edge of the church will act as edge of frame.

Odd-Geir, Linus (focus puller) and I climb aboard the cherry picker. The ride is bumpy and a bit scary. Up there it's obvious the crowd is too small for there to be any real benefit in the shot. We take it anyway. Who knows?

We get down to *terra firma* and Jelena (script supervisor) lets us know that there were lots of manholes and iron railings in shot. Good: I won't even have to look at the shot in the edit.

We do the whole sequence of the demonstration again: the crowd singing and finishing with chants of "Lietuva, Lietuva, Lietuva." It's now Marija's (Sofija) turn to address the crowd. After Gediminas's strong performance I am anxious, but Marija is incredible. I look at her on the monitor, and she steps back and breathes in as she delivers yet another paragraph of bile against the Russian Empire. She is fantastic. The extras are spontaneously ecstatic at her delivery and message and applaud loudly.

I focus on Marija in the same way as I did with Gediminas and both she and the extras are hoarse. But she is truly brilliant. Already I recognise my naiveté: it will be on the performances like Marija's that the film will possibly succeed.

I decide to try the horse one more time, but without Nikolaj in the saddle. He can stand alongside as the stunt rider (in Russian military uniform) does his work. This time we try the sequence *without* gunfire, and instead rely simply on Nikolaj's command. The soldiers are also instructed to pull two speakers off the podium and leave Sofija where she is.

We do this 4 or 5 times with the following results: the horse knocks over a few people; the soldiers engage in hand-to-hand combat with the extras; Gediminas hurts his knee; and we avoid some modern fixtures and fittings on surrounding walls, but not all of them.

I finish with 3 short sequences: firstly, a shot of Sofija looking forlorn and then turning to 'face' Nikolaj; a close up of Nikolaj; and finally, and with great difficulty, I ask some extras to weep and cry at the consequences of the attack. It's difficult, but one man does a great visual display of pain and horror. Jelena, the script supervisor, tells me that the man was actually speaking nonsense, but that won't matter because the scene will be subject to a musical overlay.

We thank the extras, many of who ask me why I'm interested in Lithuania, and then we head off for the next location.

Sofija (Marija Korenkaitė) at her husband's grave

So far the day has been good, but the next location presents problems. It's a scene to be shot 'day for night' when Čiurlionis tells Sofija to "look up at the stars." The location is the University Square with a nice exterior corridor. When Odd-Geir suggested the day for night there had been bright sunlight pouring in: it was now 7 o'clock in the early evening, light, but certainly not sunny. He suggested some hokum pokum with the camera but I decided to abandon the shot for another day. Artūras agreed.

The cemetery is next, for the scene whereby Sofija and two mourners sit by Čiurlionis's grave. By the time we arrive it is nicely dark and Audrius has set up the grave -a pile of earth- and a number of candles on and around it. There's also a wonderful minimalist wooden cross on top. However, there are too many candles on the ground and I ask them to spread them more widely around the grave. Odd-Geir lights the scene and we await the actors.

Marija and two extras duly arrive. All 3 wear black. We get them to kneel by the grave but Marija looks so small compared to the two men that we put her on a box, suitably disguised by her long coat. We take a shot of the three of them, low down, opposite on a slight incline. Then we shoot a pan. Then a big close up of Marija: she looks just like a head suspended in darkness. Wonderful.

We climb a small incline and take a couple of shots from above. I then decide we should have them walk away, and this we do - they walk to and past us. It works a treat.

Odd-Geir and I stop in a bar and I grimace as I witness Chelsea win the Champions League final against Bayern Munich. Chelsea - the *business* owned by an oligarch who was one day selling plastic ducks in a Moscow market, next day was worth billions of Roubles. It sickens me to witness the rise of this small group of men at the expense of workers and peasants who have had whatever little they possessed stolen from them.

May 20th

It's my day off and it's so hot I have to buy a hat. I hate hats.

12

SOME UNEXPECTED BAD NEWS

May 21st

I wake up worrying about money and the fact that this week should seal our destiny.

Today we're at the Dominican (Lukiskiu) Monastery in which later we'll be shooting a number of sanatorium scenes. However, today's particular scenes are those of the interior of the *Viltis* publishing house where there's an editorial meeting in which Sofija defends her work with Dr Basanavičius, and where later she will defend herself from Rostov's sexual advances.

The interior of this small monastery room is wonderful. There are 4 desks, and a 150 year-old mechanical printing press, sourced by Audrius and brought to the location with great difficulty: indeed, I cannot see they could have possibly got it through the windows. But they did.

An extra will work the press, another extra will be a journalist, but the main action will be with Sofija, the editor (Eugenijus Ignatavičius) and another journalist (Artūras Sužiedėlis). Eugenijus has a quite wonderful face. As the script supervisor-continuity person, Jelena, suggests, he *really* looks out of 1908. It's more than his costume, just something about him.

We do some nice sequences with the printing press, typewriter, pens etc., and then we have to abort the first main shot because Jelena notices that Eugenijus is wearing a small hearing aid. Neither Odd-Geir nor I had noticed this. There was then a lengthy discussion about whether or not a particular pen he was using was *period*. It was concluded that it was, but it nevertheless looked so new we abandon it.

The shooting of the scene was pretty uneventful except that we could see the hands of a clock suggesting early morning when it should have been later in the day.

At the completion of the scene Eugenijus shook my hand and spoke to me in Lithuanian as if I knew what he was talking about.

We rearrange a few things for the next scene. Nikolaj has entered the building unnoticed because, unlike the previous Saturday, he's not wearing a Russian officer's uniform, but instead he wears a baseball cap, bright almost Day-Glo shorts and trainers.

We have an early lunch (13:45) and I talk with Marija and Nikolaj. I stress, especially to Nikolaj, that his character has many sides and that he isn't just a Russian bastard. He gets the drift. Marija asks a couple of questions and then I leave them to talk to each other. I am in awe of Marija's ability to perform so many (quite different) scenes, at high intensity, in one short day. She doesn't ever complain, just gets on with it.

Artūras says he wants a word. It transpires that tomorrow's outside shoot at Užutrakio -Chekhov play, boats on the lake, walk in the forest, etc.- will have to be rearranged. Some cock up somewhere. "Okay we'll do something else," I murmur, and Artūras sets out to sort the problem. I can tell Marija is a little anxious. I ask whether she wants to see any of Saturday's rushes. She's very keen so I find Tomas, the DIT (Digital Image Transfer) man, and we retreat to his van and computer. I show her a take of one of her speeches. There are tears in her eyes.

I am anxious about today's scene where Rostov threatens Sofija and then tries to sexually assault her. I shouldn't have been. They play it perfectly, word for word -which continues to amaze: actors speaking my own words- and with great passion. Indeed, the final scene where Sofija dissolves into tears is quite terrific. Very moving.

We finish 5 hours earlier than scheduled, so I seek out Artūras to discuss scheduling: perhaps we are quicker than the usual teams, or perhaps we simply spend less time on lighting. I also think it helps that I am not Lithuanian, so there's less knowledge about me and fewer things to gossip about.

Artūras says we will film the 8-page scene in the library tomorrow. This will be a 'big day.' It's been moved forward a day.

I walk back to the apartment in the balmy heat, somewhere around 30 degrees, and feel that a) that it has been a good day's work, and b) that editing in a foreign language will be more difficult than I imagine.

I send Marija an email and a still from the cemetery. I add, "thank you, I'm so lucky you're in the film." She replies a few hours later -Kylie Minogue style- that, "No, thank you. I'm so lucky, lucky, lucky, that I'm in your film."

May 22nd

Get up early and go to the office, via the cash machine where I withdraw some more money. At the office Artūras tells me that the money is needed for extras and actors.

Today is a big set up - about 17 windows to black out in the beautiful Vilnius University Special Collections Library, resplendent with frescos on the ceiling. This is the scene that sets up the film: Čiurlionis meets Sofija for the first time, and where she also encounters Captain Rostov. In addition, significantly, it is where Sofija discusses the need to protect the Lithuanian language.

I've longed to start this scene with a tilt down from the fresco to the Chairman of the meeting who at this evening meeting

Some extras at the Vilnius University Special Collections Library

introduces Sofija who, as mentioned, is to speak about the need to retain and protect the Lithuanian language.

It takes quite a while to light, of course, and then the extras are wheeled in. They look fabulous, in the sense that they look 'period': however, they do *also* look like 20 undertakers.

We set up the shot, but first take some singles from the fresco - Christ, his father, angels, etc. Then we do the tilt down on the men at the meeting, talking and coughing, etc. I precisely time it so that just as we reach the Chairman -standing at the end of a long table- he's introducing Sofija, who then stands. It works perfectly, although I do it 3 times to make sure.

We move the camera and begin to cover Sofija's little speech. I've got Rostov opposite her and Čiurlionis on *her* side of the table, just a few seats down. Everything is working well. Sofija starts by refusing to speak Polish, instead, "I'll speak the language of my Fatherland." It goes well, until sometimes casually remarks to me, "shouldn't the Chairman have introduced her in Polish?" I feel like throwing the proverbial dummy out the pram. No one had told me that he wasn't actually speaking Polish. I checked with the script and the translator had omitted to translate his introduction. So I'll have to do *all* those shots again.

We do the usual stuff: cutaways of men listening, Nikolaj's speech, Rokas's speech, reverse angles etc., then have another perplexing discussion about the "axis," which I understand in theory but find the issue more perplexing when actually on set - and with time against me.

We get the Polish translation for the 2 sentences (from Artūras's Polish wife, luckily available at the end of a telephone) and reshoot the introduction to the scene.

We're about to break for lunch when Odd-Geir decides that he wants to take a still. He sets it up but Monica (wardrobe-on-set) gets in shot and he tells her to "fuck off." I ask him, "what's wrong? Why are you behaving like that?" He says he hates it when he gets "arrogant." I suggest he apologises to Monica.

Lunch. Then another big set up at the other end of the room where there's an after-meeting conversation and then the interaction firstly between Rostov and Sofija, and then Čiurlionis and Sofija. The first thing we do is a set up with conversations between various groups of men around the 3 main characters, with waitresses dispensing food and drink, and so on. This works well especially when Odd-Geir puts the camera on his shoulder and takes some intimate shots.

Sofija (Marija Korenkaitė) is cornered by Captain Rostov (Nikolaj Antonov)

Then when we start the sequence when Rostov approaches Sofija, the trouble begins. First, he's too slow and no matter how many times I suggest he should move a little quicker, he simply appears to find it too difficult. Then there's the issue of the wooden floor: when their dialogue begins it's as if someone is jumping up and down on the floorboards. Artūras (props-on-set) brings some blankets but it still doesn't solve the problem. I ask them *all* to take off their shoes. We do the Rostov-Sofija piece, but it isn't perfect. But okay.

There's then a little choreography to arrange when Čiurlionis arrives and eases Rostov diplomatically away. I don't get it quite right, am worried about the time, and Odd-Geir sarcastically remarks that, "some directors rehearse, Mr Mullan." He's quite right of course, and I'm certainly not giving the focus puller enough time to make his marks on the floor.

We manage to sort it out and shoot a nice piece of dialogue between our leads. It's nice because they laugh easily with one another and they convey the idea that they're already falling in love.

After 10 hours we're ready to go outside and do the shot we aborted on May 19, when Sofija walks away from this very same meeting and Čiurlionis suggests that she, "looks up at the stars." It's helpful that they're in the right costumes, so that saves time.

It's shot along a long corridor, lit as if the moon is shining in. We do it a few times, mainly to ensure that she's not in shadow when Rokas calls out to her. Finally, we take advantage of the fact that we're outside the wonderful St. John's Church (situated within the University courtyard) to put the camera on the baby legs and look up at the church from behind her head/hat. It works well, but what works even better and is when we stand on the scaffolding and shoot her looking up to "the stars." After one take I ask her to finish with a smile. She does. I'm happy.

Odd-Geir and I have a gira on the way home and exchange views. I said I thought he was unnecessarily sarcastic at times, he said I was rushing things. We're both right.

May 23rd

The first set up is in a courtyard where Sofija is caught by Rostov after leaving the demonstration she was speaking at. It works well but I notice that Nikolaj says, "come to Moscow," when it should be St. Petersburg. So we do it again.

In-between takes, Odd-Geir's phone rings and he speaks to someone in his native Norwegian. Afterwards the blood disappears from his face and he is white. It materialises that he'd had some blood tests taken in Oslo after the St. Petersburg shooting and he'd just been told that given the high PSA reading in the blood he *might* have prostate cancer. He disappears for a walk. I discreetly tell Artūras.

Odd-Geir returns and we do the shot where Rostov and Sofija first kiss. It's good. They'd suggested one script change and I'd gratefully agreed to their initiative.

We're early for the next set-up, so Odd-Geir, Artūras and I go for a coffee. Odd-Geir explains that the Norwegian doctor says that he urgently requires a scan. Artūras arranges one for 7 o'clock, same day, at the American Baltic Clinic.

It's grim.

The next scene is a short one (1/8 page) when some Russian soldiers drag Catholics out of their homes. We found a great location, a small courtyard where at the top of an apartment is a Madonna figure, behind which, we can shoot.

All this takes time, especially as the extras take a long time to understand what's required. I notice that at 11.00 in the morning one of them is demonstrably and exceedingly *drunk*.

Nikolaj struts his stuff, barks out orders to his troops and they run up stairs and drag away some Catholics. Job done.

Linus (focus puller), Odd-Geir and I quickly go to the Church of the Holy Spirit to shoot a little GV.

Lunch. Odd-Geir is clearly distressed, and we've a lengthy set of scenes ahead of us at the café Skonis ir Kvapas.

The café scenes aren't straightforward, especially as we don't have many extras. I'm also meeting Ramunė Skardžiunaitė for only the second time, having cast her in very quick time. She plays Sofija's mother. And then there's Odd-Geir and his situation.

We start with a master shot with lots of movement, with a waiter walking up and down the café. Then we do some close-ups, two shots of cups going to mouths, etc. We then start the dialogue between Sofija and Čiurlionis. This goes well although, because I know him so well, I'm always a little uncomfortable watching Rokas. I oscillate between wanting him to just be himself and for him to 'be' Čiurlionis. But it all works well. Then Jelena -script supervisor- talks to both Rokas and I and discusses a Lithuanian word. They argue and argue and argue, and my head spins. The translation issue is raising its ugly head on an almost daily basis. Yesterday, for example, after we stopped filming the Rostov-Sofija scene it was pointed out to me that the Russian translation had missed out the sentence, "As your whore?" and just translated, "I'm not for sale." I thought I could live with that, but now I'm regretting that I didn't re-shoot it, and wonder what other horrors await me.

We shoot the reverses, and then do some nice close ups of Rokas scribbling away at a music score. Gedrius (boom operator) seems to be particularly enjoying the sound of the scratching of the pencil.

It's now time for Odd-Geir to go for a scan, so we just announce a break.

He returns after 90 minutes. Artūras tells me the scan reveals cancer and that the next step is a biopsy to confirm the extent of this. This has been arranged for Monday, the day we are to shoot Čiurlionis's wedding, reception and funeral. I don't know whether to laugh or cry.

I've already a Plan B. If Odd-Geir decides to simply go home to Oslo I'll ask Tomas the DIT man to operate (if he's agreeable). He is a DOP, young, speaks good English and works regularly with Linus, the focus puller.

I have a discreet word with Odd-Geir. "Are you going back to Oslo tonight?" He makes it clear in his usual grumpy way that he wants to stay - "besides, medical treatment here is quicker than in Norway." I tell him, truthfully, that whatever works for him is okay with me.

We shoot Sofija's dialogue with her mother. Ramune, who plays Mrs Kymantaitė, overacts a little. Probably my fault, as I offer her no instructions or advice. So I have a discreet word, and it takes a while for her to settle down but then it all works well.

It's late and we go home, via a restaurant. I need a gira, and so order one. The waitress -not one of God's brightest creatures- brings me the homemade version, with alcohol and with fat raisins. Instead, I ask for a gira from a bottle. "You want a bottle to pour it in?" "No, I want the gira from a bottle." "So, I'll pour this into a bottle?" It goes on like this for a while until we eventually understand each other.

I don't know what to say to Odd-Geir over and above the usual platitudes - "Who knows how serious it might be?" "I've heard that men die *with* prostate cancer not *because* of it," etc.

May 24th

We've got Odd-Geir another medical appointment on our day off, this time with the country's leading urologist. It's at 17.00 hours.

I'm in the office all day trying to raise money. Still no news from Eversheds. I hook up with a man called Geoffrey Cohn who is an Englishman and long-time Vilnius resident. He suggests some people that I might contact.

I wait by the phone.

Odd-Geir returns from the hospital and says that he's had a physical examination and that the doctor thinks its stage 3 cancer. We manage to get a biopsy for tomorrow, at 08.00 in the morning.

May 25th

06:00 Odd-Geir gets up, having not slept, blames me, and rants and raves. Then leaves for the hospital.

07:00. Odd-Geir calls from the hospital and apologies for his "unacceptable" behaviour. I tell him not to worry.

Today we're marching Russian troops through the Old Town. After that I can't remember what we are supposed to be doing and I feel totally unprepared.

Odd-Geir turns up at 10.15, right on time, biopsy duly performed. He doesn't want to talk about it.

The first shot takes a little longer then I expect: marching soldiers in a square. They're slovenly and don't look like crack Russian troops. But Artūras helps get them into shape. We fix the shot, do it 3 or 4 times, and then Odd-Geir wants to use his Canon 5 device and does so. I have no idea how it'll turn out.

Off now to Literatu g, a windy slightly hilly street in the Old Town, which has a huge tattoo shop as one of its features! Audrius has dressed it beautifully, and it is the perfect location.

While we're waiting for the troops I tell Artūras that I want to re-shoot the "whore" scene. He agrees.

The troops stomp down the hill and the extras duly move out of the way when they approach. One of the extras looks uncannily like a younger V I Lenin. I tell him and he says, "cool."

Marija is also walking down the hill, reading a letter from Čiurlionis, and as usual, she's perfect. Correct pace, correct expression. We change the lens to the 400mm and the shot's even better.

The rest of the day is spent re-creating Vilnius 1908 street scenes. Stiklai Street is usually one of over-priced boutiques aimed at tourists (especially Americans), but Audrius et al., have covered the ground in some sort of sand, changed signs and added nice, small, period features.

The first set up involves people walking along the street while soldiers frisk them and actively engage in fighting one shop owner. The shop owner and the soldiers get stuck in and many props -bone china, glasses, plates- get inadvertently broken. Some of the other extras are a little wooden despite my best efforts at rousing them. I realise that this is another of my directorial weaknesses.

I then break for lunch and eat with everyone else including soldiers and other extras in a courtyard. I begin to notice the faces of the extras: it's a small country and there aren't enough to go around. I see two older ladies with beaten faces and I realise they would do well for the St. Petersburg voice over sequence (Sofija: "mama, there's so much poverty here"). I mention this to Renata (wardrobe) and she sends for some Russian headscarves. I get the camera, tell them not to smile, and take the shots. They will work well with Marija's voice over. Over lunch I decide I need a violinist -preferably Jewish- to play in the street scene, in order to add colour. Jurga says she'll look at her casting database.

I get all the extras onto the street, plus a few soldiers *sans* rifles. Some of the extras are selling bread, others mending shoes and so on. They walk up and down, do a little selling, but it's a bit flat. Then, a mere 90 minutes after making the request, my violinist turns up, dressed and made-up. He's 82 with a wonderful face. Gedrius sticks a microphone in his hat and off we go. He adds life to the event.

Artūras's six-year-old son, Davidas, is also present and is genuinely cute. I try and use him in these street scenes, but some of these scenes just don't work, and so I have to find a way of improving them.

I notice, again, a man with a long black and white beard, and huge piercing eyes. I ask him whether he could tell Davidas and two small girls a story. Yes he can. We shoot it tight and from two points of view. It is incredible. It's like the Devil speaking to children. The story he tells is a traditional fairy tale about a clockmaker. I've shot more than enough of this -in fact I'm indulging myself- and it comes to an end when the storyteller asks Davidas a question and even I recognise a word in his response - "Maxima [the supermarket]." Everyone laughs. We finish.

The day ends with a short scene with a pregnant Sofija, alongside Mr Dobuzhinsky, approaching the exterior of a dilapidated 'St. Petersburg' apartment. It's short and sweet.

13

BABUSHKAS AND BANKRUPTCY

May 26th

Up early for a set of sequences at the 'sanatorium' near the Polish border. It is quite chilly. The location is Vingis Park, a huge area of forest, parkland, small zoo and stadium. Indeed Lady Gaga follows us in a couple of weeks. The entrance is partially blocked and we discover there's a marathon due to end there. No one told me, so I'm a little perturbed.

First up are Dobuzhinsky and Sofija arriving at the sanatorium, then a scene with Sofija and her mother also arriving, with newborn baby, Danūtė. For this scene only, we use a doll. It's been hanging around the office for a few days and is spookily lifelike.

These scenes are quickly done. The next scene requires 'patients' to roam around the sanatorium gardens. The trouble is I only have two of them, so I ask Pilius -my 'assistant'- to get dressed and be an extra patient. He does this willingly and the costumers in the parked van speedily turn him into a sick man. With his short-cropped hair and shot in close-up, he looks like a refugee or concentration camp inmate.

These scenes with the two nurses -who, sadly and irritatingly, can't be seen together as they are *sharing* one costume- are carried out quickly.

Next up Rokas has to hug Dobuzhinsky who has been to see him in the sanatorium and is about to leave. Andrius, who plays Dobuzhinsky, is a serious and professional actor who plays it perfectly: as he hugs Čiurlionis goodbye he rests his head gently on Rokas's shoulder. The shot lingers on Rokas, in big close-up, and lo and behold a tear is squeezed out.

Čiurlionis then sits with a nurse and shows her a lock of Danūtė's hair that he's just received in the post from Sofija. A ribbon in a card sticks the hair, with a message alongside (to be voice-overed by Sofija). Rokas points out that Sofija does not sign it, and in 1908 people of her class would have written their name. Artūras (props-on-set) is called and he fishes out the appropriate pen from his box of tricks, but no one knows her signature. So for the close-up of the card we have to use Rokas's fingers to hide the missing signature.

Again Rokas is very good, but I'm slightly annoyed at the cock-up.

We now face a race against time: if we're not at the main gate in 20 minutes it'll close for the next 4 hours to allow all the marathon runners in.

After successfully escaping the park, we drive back into town to Traku Street where the next location is a Jewellery shop in St. Petersburg. In fact it is opposite the café Skonis ir Kvapas at which we shot some scenes 3 days earlier: they share a common courtyard. It's a nice simple exterior. Čiurlionis and Dobuzhinsky approach the door and enter, with some extras walking past them. I never quite get the choreography right, but it's passable. Lunch.

Čiurlionis is going to ask the jeweller for 2 rings engraved with astrological symbols. The Russian translation has "astronomical symbols," as opposed to the zodiac term. So, more anxiety: what else is wrong? We spend time going over the Russian translation and find more mistakes.

The jeweller is Aleksandr Lichačiov, a strong-looking Russian actor and he possesses a perfect face. Grey hair, sharp eyes, open smile. I decide to do quite a lot with him on his own, especially as Audrius has dressed the shop perfectly. So, we use a magnifying glass for him to examine rings and necklaces. We shoot him with at least two different lenses.

We subsequently have to shoot the Rokas and Dobuzhinsky scene quite a few times, because Jelena (script supervisor) keeps telling me that Rokas is getting his Russian wrong. It's the second alien language he's used today -Polish in the sanatorium, then this- so it's hardly surprising. Eventually he gets it right. The scene is necessary, although not awe-inspiring, either visually or in terms of meaning. However, the jeweller examining the rings and bracelets is rich in detail.

Only once, and in frustration, Rokas tells me to "shut up." He is not, I hope, turning into a prima donna.

I get Artūras (props-on-set) to move some necklaces and we shoot some jewellery from Dobuzhinsky's point of view. Finally, and a little to everyone's annoyance, I ask everyone to prepare for a shot behind the jeweller: everything (including furniture) has to be moved. But the shot works really well.

Kestas drops by, with his daughter, and we agree to meet (with Artūras [production manager] and Rokas) tomorrow to discuss our financial problems. I do sometimes laugh to myself when I hear film makers talk of their crises when they're working with budgets of £1m-£40m. This film will cost about £250,000 in cash and, hopefully, will look on-screen a £2m+ film.

We're looking for relatively small amounts of cash but perhaps surprisingly, no one is interested in helping us.

We move from the jewellery shop into the heart of the Old Town, to the Pilies Street Art Gallery. This is a nice location, with numerous internal arches. It's owned by a thirty-something woman, a gift from her wealthy minor-oligarch husband. She greets us and says she's invited a magazine photographer to take some shots of us all together (with her).

There are two scenes to be shot here: one where Dobuzhinsky discusses with Čiurlionis the prevalence of angels in his paintings and another where Čiurlionis defends his paintings against his critics.

I'm already a little fazed after seeing Kestas earlier, and now it's made worse when Artūras suggests to Rokas and I that we all meet after today's shoot to discuss how to approach Kestas, and what our party line should be.

The first scene with Dobuzhinsky is shot without too much fuss.

For the second, longer scene, I get 7 extras to wander through the gallery. This they do, although too quietly for my liking. I get a couple of them to look at a painting, and kind of discuss it. Then we set up Rokas (Čiurlionis) and two critics, one of whom looks uncannily like Eddie Izzard (a man who always fails to make me laugh). The scene works well: Rokas improvises about the painting, *Evening*, because the one I'd asked to be copied, *Night*, hadn't been. 'Eddie' was especially good, snarling at Rokas as he tells him there's no need to try and explore life's mysteries in his paintings because only God does that.

At the end of the shoot the gallery owner tells Artūras that she'd like to buy the replica Čiurlionis paintings. He lets me know. She also tells him that there are people with money she knows who *may* be able to help with the film. I've heard it all before, but who knows?

It's a 'wrap' and everyone is pleased that we've finished early. Artūras, Rokas and I find a small bar, drink some gira, and discuss our 'strategy.'

We begin to reiterate what we know: a) we are short of cash, b) that Rokas's mother's life savings are coming our way, and c) I am continuing to pay £750 a day of my own dwindling supply of money to help keep things afloat. And: that we are waiting to hear from Eversheds and other possible investors and sponsors.

I leave the meeting with a sense of doom, increased when I spend the rest of the evening in a cafe watching the *Eurovision Song Contest* with a) Englebert Humperdinck looking 100 years-old, despite his evident and obvious cosmetic surgery, b) the Russian babushkas, and c) the Lithuanian entry, a young man singing in English. I immediately think of Sofija's speech in the library when she talks of the need to cherish the Lithuanian language.

I later learn that the babushkas were singing "let's party, let's do it," despite all of them looking 60+ and one of them unquestionably in her late 80's. I later learned that they had a 'B team' in place in case any of them fell ill or dropped-dead on the show. Bizarre.

On the streets people say "hello" -strangers, people I don't know- then I realise they are extras I've encountered on the film.

14

THE MAN FROM *THE MATRIX*

Meet up with Kestas et al. and he informs us that he's "technically bankrupt." After a lengthy conversation -and, surprisingly, not too argumentative- we agree that the film *has* to be completed. I promise that at the end of the film -if Eversheds et al. do not help- I will personally find the £100,000 to pay any outstanding bills. From where, God only knows. Meanwhile, Artūras will talk to the crew about this promise of mine.

We leave. Rokas and I laugh -darkly?- about him asking his mother for her life savings. She's 70 and has no substantial pension.

I tell him that for tomorrow's wedding reception, to be shot at the Pushkin Museum, I need a *working* piano. We decide to go and look again at the piano (the Becker). We're allowed in to the Museum by the surly Russian woman who acts as gatekeeper: and, as we expected, the piano doesn't work. In fact the keys are almost totally frozen.

We locate a working piano through Rokas's wife, Sonata, and it will be delivered at 08:00 in the morning.

The Old Town is full of singers and dancers in traditional costume. It's a kind of Bulgarian-choirs-meet-Morris-dancers event.

All innocent, and quietly patriotic. However, it's spoiled by a group of English stag tourists, all drunk, shouting abuse at them.

May 28th

I wake up early seething about something happened on Saturday afternoon at the art gallery. Odd-Geir likes to use broken mirrors to light some scenes (in combination, of course, with traditional lighting). The trouble is that for the viewer the effect might lead them to think that we've forgotten to move one of the lamps. So, Odd-Geir wants to use one of these broken mirrors for the shot with Čiurlionis and Dobuzhinsky. I don't like it and I gently tell him so. He rounds on me and screams, "Am I lighting this, or you?" This is both totally unnecessary and absolutely unprofessional, especially when done in front of the rest of the cast and crew. None of us are perfect but his bad temper and prima donna tendencies annoy me. I am tired of treading on eggshells around him.

Being a director and trying to keep everyone happy is not easy.

Today's schedule sees Čiurlionis get married in the morning and then a few hours later in the evening, buried.

The first location is the Jerusalem Church, a location I've lusted after for years. It has a lengthy set of steps that the happy couple et al. can walk down, picked off with precision by our 400mm lens. The shot works well, although Rokas continues to smile a little a little too much for my liking.

Then we're off to the Pushkin Museum for the wedding reception. I decide to shoot the exterior 'farewells' first, as the weather is still fine, matches the wedding ceremony, and we might as well get it over as soon as possible. It works well, except Vaidotas, the actor who plays Sofija's father, overdoes the drunken role I suggest he takes.

Inside the Museum the Russian curator watches us closely. We're not to work in certain areas, not to touch certain things, there's plastic sheeting all over the floor, and so on.

Wedding party with Čiurlionis's father (Vidas Petkevičius) and Sofija (Marija Korenkaitė)

The first shot is an establishing shot of the wedding party, with children -including Artūras's son, Davidas, lively with a loud voice- and we tilt up from the table, which is splendidly dressed with food and drink, and across the faces. Some of the actors aren't relaxed enough, and Čiurlionis's sister Juzefa repeatedly looks at the camera. But we easily get more than enough material.

Next we do a close up on the champagne bottle being opened, but discover that there's a plastic top under the foil. We break for lunch, send out for a real cork top, and plan the next shot.

I get special treatment for lunch as I'm a) the director and b) possibly the sole vegetarian on the shoot. Usually it's some black bread and cheese, which suits me fine, followed by some fruit.

Today it's 4 white rolls and almost an *orchard* of apples. I hate taking some of the food back as the caterer always looks so offended and hurt, so I look for the children to share the fruit.

We re-shoot the champagne shot, and it goes well. Now it is Rokas's turn to play the piano: the sequence is for him to stop the celebrations and announce that he wants to play some music for his *mothers*, *fathers* and, of course, Sofija. Then he plays the short pieces and adds something at the end.

This all goes well and we reverse the shot, etc. I then record all the music with Zigitas and Gedrius to ensure we have a clean track.

The 'adds something at the end' turns out to be a Lithuanian folk tune *Ant kalno gluosnys* (and I manage to get the cast to sing it as Rokas plays). We then print out the words on paper for those unsure of the lyrics. The singing is fulsome, especially from Eugenijus Ignatavičius, one of the wedding guests, and who plays Sofija's editor at *Viltis*, the newspaper.

It really is a heart-warming scene.

Next up are Rokas and Sofija dancing, with Jonas - Čiurlionis's little brother – playing the Lithuanian folk tune, mentioned earlier. I don't expect this to go well, but it does, with Rokas pulling Sofija onto the floor dancing. Other couples follow suit and they move back and forward towards the camera. The editor gets involved, until we notice his hearing device, so we have to re-shoot. Then we shoot Jonas playing the piano, the children listening and, all in all, it is much better than I'd imagined.

I have a feeling – but I could be naïve of course – that these Lithuanian actors enjoy being in a film which is about traditional Lithuanian culture. Many current Lithuanian films are gangster films based on US-type formats.

I tell everyone we can go to the next location and then discover there's a short scene with Sofija reading a letter in her apartment (also located in the Pushkin Museum). We wait for her to change into the appropriate dress and then shoot the scene. I just do one take.

The funeral scene is something I've been dreading, partly because of anxieties about noise from surrounding roads, but also because of fears that I may not be able to get the actors to do what I would like them to do.

The actors are late (from the Pushkin) so we shoot a nice cutaway of the cross. The actors arrive and we put them in place. The priest -played by Rolandas Boravskis- is a sensational looking man, with a touch of Mongolia about him. When he's wandering around the set in his black cassock, Ray-Bans, and iPad he looks like something from the *Matrix*.

In this scene Nikolaj approaches Sofija at the end of the funeral and expresses his condolences. She rebuffs him. So Nikolaj steps forward and instead of "Sofija" he says "Marija" so it's more shooting, as the clock ticks towards overtime.

The final shots are some singles and pans. There's a great shot of Čiurlionis's grieving parents and behind them, a few metres away, Nikolaj. The extreme-close-up of Sofija is terrific. She has a face for all occasions.

On the drive to the office Artūras asks me if I'll get some more money out so we can pay extras in cash, to save taxes etc., and we also discuss the fact that Eversheds have been in touch saying they're still discussing things; that the Vilnius Mayor's office has been in touch requesting a meeting; and other money related matters.

I am so tired.

15

DRUSKININKAI

Druskininkai is where Čiurlionis spent most of his childhood. It is well known for that fact and also for its spas and sanatoria - very popular with Poles, Belarusians, Lithuanians and Russians. Today we're driving there for some sequences at the actual house where he and his parents and 8 siblings lived.

May 29th

We drive there in convoy - I'm with Artūras. Odd-Geir is with his wife (on a short visit) and Rokas with Valentinas, the main driver. We stop at the first garage in Vilnius and meet Gena (gaffer) and crew, Linus (focus puller) and crew, and Artūras (props-on-set) and crew, and we all stock up on fuel courtesy of Artūras's petrol card.

Druskininkai Municipality is the only Lithuanian organisation to help us: they were going to pay 30,000 Litas (now reduced to 10,000), pay for meals and accommodation for one night. So we are grateful.

The drive is uneventful: Artūras and I share similar perceptions as to the conflicts with partners over child rearing and other such matters. I am becoming really fond of him.

The first meal the Municipality provide for us is in a sanatorium. It is a splendid rest and recuperation dwelling. Large, with many residents -most, but not all, elderly- and with a nice waitressed three-course lunch.

The first sequence is a GV outside the 2 wooden houses that constitute the Čiurlionis family home. We use 4 children, the "siblings," including Rytis Juškaitis who plays Čiurlionis's brother Povilas. They play around the house but it's tame stuff. I also sense that Odd-Geir's a bit grumpy. Anyhow, we do it and conclude with a nice shot of Povilas (aged about 16 in the film) reading a book (Nietzsche, as it happens).

The next shot sees Čiurlionis (Rokas) talking with his parents and sister, Juzefa. His father shares with him the fact that since he lost his job as the Church organist (because he wouldn't speak Polish) he's short of money. Čiurlionis says he'll give more music lessons, but his mother is only interested in his new love interest - Sofija. We're going to shoot it in a nice little conservatory-type part of the house. I am so a) inexperienced and b) so aware of the deteriorating weather and related time issues, that I don't rehearse and so Odd-Geir gives me one of his rants: "we can't get this right if you don't fucking rehearse." He's right, of course, but his frequent rants simply make me feel tense around him. He could be more diplomatic, like I am. I don't rant and rave every time he doesn't see something in the shot (post-1908 objects like hearing aids, CCTV cameras, etc.).

Anyway, we rehearse it and on the second or third take it's good. I take Odd-Geir to one side and tell him my thoughts about his rants. He says it's only because he's frustrated. We move on.

Now we move inside the house and prepare for a complicated piece of piano playing with Rokas and his brother, Povilas (Rytis). It's a scene that Rokas has changed a little, and he's a bit precious about it. At one stage I have to tell him that none of the other actors ever complain about my suggestions. *Only him*. At times he becomes the prima donna. But I really love him as a friend and forgive him. *However*, I have to remind him 2 more times not to have such a fixed smile. He again disagreed. So now I take him outside and give him a bollocking. He subsequently sulks, but I'm sick of it and don't care.

We do the scene where Čiurlionis eventually plays a four-hander with Povilas, from Greig. It is nice. I do have to get quite a few facial expressions (as cutaways) from Povilas because he's a little one-dimensional. Of course, it doesn't help that he wears non-removable orthodontic braces, hence limiting his facial movements. Rokas asked that I cast him, because he was an accomplished pianist (who could therefore be taught to play *poorly*), but had overlooked the braces. Another sign of my too-easy-going-weak-nature.

Rokas paints next (*The Sun Passing Through the Sign of Virgo*) and Audrius (art director) has got someone to produce a good copy of the original painting. Odd-Geir -with his experience from the *Munch* film- gets some good shots from a potentially limited scene.

It's taken 5 or 6 hours and I'm tired, and really fucking tired of prima donnas.

We're off now to the forest to do a scene that is scheduled for later in the shoot but which I want to do while in Druskininkai.

Čiurlionis and his father walk in the forest and discuss the Lithuanian idea that if you count the number of cuckoo sounds you hear you will learn the length of years you will live. And, of course, in the script we hear the cuckoo sound 35 times. His father laughs off the number: "It was just a game I played with you when you were a child, to amuse you."

It's now raining and Odd-Geir is again grumpy. I find a good place to walk. He says, "ok, so tell me, what lens we will use?" He always chooses the appropriate lens so I know he's trying to be a smart-arse. I say 400mm, and he agrees. The shot is great and

-miracles do happen- just when they say "listen," a cuckoo sings.

We eat under a tent and prepare for the final 2 shots of the day. I'm bitten alive by all the forest insects.

The final 2 shots focus on Čiurlionis's walk in the forest when he's at the sanatorium where he subsequently gets wet by the rain, lies down, catches pneumonia and dies. The first shot involves water towers, which are assembled by 3 extraordinary men - straight from a Coen brother's film. The slick and smooth one, the pony-tailed hippy-cum-hit man, and the beer bellied one who manages to speak fluently while smoking.

We get wet: Rokas gets wet, we get the shot, as he walks through the forest. Then the final shot is where he lies in a foetal position on the ground. It's a nicely composed shot but as we mark the slate an ant crawls into Rokas's ear. We re-set and shoot. It is good.

Čiurlionis (Rokas Zubovas) and his father (Vidas Petkevičius) in the Druskininkai forest.

Our Municipality-provided *accommodation* is in fact a few trailers on a camping site. Our's -Rokas, Artūras and me- has no hot water and I am already cold with wet feet from the forest. It doesn't dampen the spirits of everyone else and we sit outside in some wooden hut-cum-canopy in the rain drinking cans of lager and gira. There's much laughter and considerable camaraderie. I go to bed at 01:00, while Rokas and Artūras come 'home' at 04:00.

16

BABY BOYS, BABY GIRLS

Breakfast is at the café in the Aqua Park Hotel. It is absolutely perfect, highly tasty, edible and well served: then we're off back to Vilnius to kill some Catholics.

The location is the church at Rykantai, a great location in one sense as it is on a slight hill and surrounded only by greenery, however, the downside is that it's near a railway line.

The first scene has some soldiers dragging two men out of a bell tower. We have to rehearse this a few times as all involved are extras. The consolation is that there are bells (of course) in the bell tower and they alone give us some good shots.

Then we establish a mother and son - a young man who will later be shot and die in his mother's arms. That's the plan anyway.

Next up are the lengthy scenes - with extras, with the exception of Nikolaj (Rostov) and Rolandas (the priest) who looks uncannily like Yul Brunner from the *King and I*.

The scenes seem to be taking forever and have to be choreographed in an extremely complicated way. I'm out of my depth, but we struggle on.

We get to the point where we have to use rifles and shoot people.

I've decided against fake blood, as it looks absurd on low budget films. Besides 'blood' alone trivialises death, I believe. And, moreover, this is all new to me!

I've begun to think of our 4 victims as the 4 stooges because they are very comic and wooden. But we slowly but surely amass lots of cutaways -rifles being shot, Nikolaj barking out orders, a close up of a *Bible* and some rosary beads, crosses, women's faces, etc.- and I think the scene will be less *Monty Python* and more as I hope it will be.

We finish at 18.00, after beginning at 11:45, so we've achieved a lot in those hours.

One final bit of shooting has to be undertaken today: the re-shoot of the mistranslated dialogue where the word "whore" was omitted. It involves Nikolaj and Marija. It's at the university courtyard, facing St. John's Church, and we have to put a lamp up. Marija jumps up and down on the spot either to get warm or psyche herself up.

The shot is a close-up so there's no set dressing involved. They do the scene really well, except I hear voices in the headphones and discover it's the caterer and a couple of sparks around the corner. We re-shoot and it's even better, with lots of malevolence followed by passion. End of day.

Odd-Geir gets confirmation he has prostate cancer and is told he will have a bone scan next Monday.

Rokas calls and says he is "broken hearted." I ask why and discover that the law company, Eversheds, have said no to sponsorship because there's nothing left in their budget. If they knew this why all those meetings and conference calls?

I'm suitably depressed and go to bed. With a slight toothache.

May 31st

We start off the day shooting two scenes of people (in St. Petersburg) queuing for soup in the freezing cold. It is, of course, a bright and sunny day!

The extras do indeed look hungry and homeless and I detect a few 'drinker's noses' amongst the 20 of them. Rokas is also here as in one scene I have him dressed, with a scarf over his head exactly as in one of Čiurlionis's paintings, *Funeral Symphony VII*.

Audrius (art director) has covered a wall with a construction, which looks like a small hut, and inside are a treasure of small items - soup pots, soup bowls, wooden spoons, plates, and piping hot cabbage soup and black bread. One of the walls (wooden) hasn't been painted so I ask Artūras (props-on-set) to paint it with some kind of stain/creosote. Reluctantly he agrees to try.

The two scenes are terrific. The *babushkas* serving the soup are talkative: "eat the soup, it'll do you good" - and the customers suitably and appropriately have cabbage dripping down their chins.

I leave very pleased with the 2 hours' work, then I discover that the production designer/art director, Audrius, says he will resign because we shot inside an under-prepared set. I am astonished: I simply took advantage of a great set. A meeting is called for at the lunch break, with Kestas, Artūras (production manager), Audrius and me.

Meantime I get on with the sanatorium scenes, to be shot in the dilapidated Dominican monastery.

I have about 10 extras -playing shuffling patients- and two nurses who look like nuns. And, of course, Rokas.

The first establishing shot in the corridor goes well, especially when using one of the long lenses (300mm). Then we shoot Čiurlionis playing the piano in the ward. We've decided that he plays the Jūratė and Kastytis theme which, I think, will become the musical motif of the film. These scenes go straightforwardly well.

Then it's lunchtime and I meet with the others. I diplomatically mention that when there's a problem with set dressing -e.g., plastic champagne tops- I do not throw a tantrum. I also tell Audrius that I really, truly, liked his set for the soup people.

He sulks like a child, but eventually I am asked to shake his hand, which I do, and life resumes as normal. I am asked by Kestas to inform Audrius in advance if there are to be any changes -however small- in the schedule.

So we resume and at 14:40 I am still waiting for one of Audrius's sketches to arrive, due at 14:00! I smile the smile of the moral high ground, but would prefer to have the sketch.

We shoot the scene of Čiurlionis painting and then the scene where two nurses strap him to his bed. Again, it works well, and one of the nurses in particular appears highly cognisant with such straps.

Odd-Geir talks more than usual about his cancer, and asks about bone scans. I tell him what I know, which isn't that much.

The most challenging scenes are to come: Sofija and her mother arriving at the sanatorium and then being told that her husband is dead. And, of course, instead of a doll we have a real live baby.

We rehearse the scene without the baby, and it appears straightforward if unexciting. So we decide to run the camera just in case the baby first time round performed well (i.e., doesn't scream too much). Baby Danūtė (a girl) turns out to be a boy, quite porky, named Karolis. But luckily enough he wears a bonnet and could pass for a girl! I think. *I hope*. We're told he's only available for 2 hours so I get on with it. But he's great, and as well as the master shot we get a nice cutaway with Sofija and her mother playing with him while awaiting the doctor.

I forget - there's an earlier scene with the doctor who examines Čiurlionis and pronounces his diagnosis of pneumonia. The language is Polish and he's an amateur from the Polish Theatre Company in Vilnius. He looks a bit fierce so I ask him to remember he's a physician who (eventually) conveys tragic news to Sofija.

He's fat, and as he begins his first action -bending down with a stethoscope to examine Čiurlionis- three buttons on his waistcoat explode. So there's a period of waiting while we repair his clothes.

The scene is fine, although he is incredibly nervous.

Back to Sofija, the doctor and the tragic news that Čiurlionis is dead. The set is a small, perfectly dressed room. Marija is struggling with Polish so she pins her lines to the desk in front. We shoot across the desk and then, of course, we'll do the reverses (the doctor and Sofija).

I've told Marija to do what she feels is right. So she screams, quite a lot, and disarmingly.

Scene over. Back to the office and the continuation of the search for money.

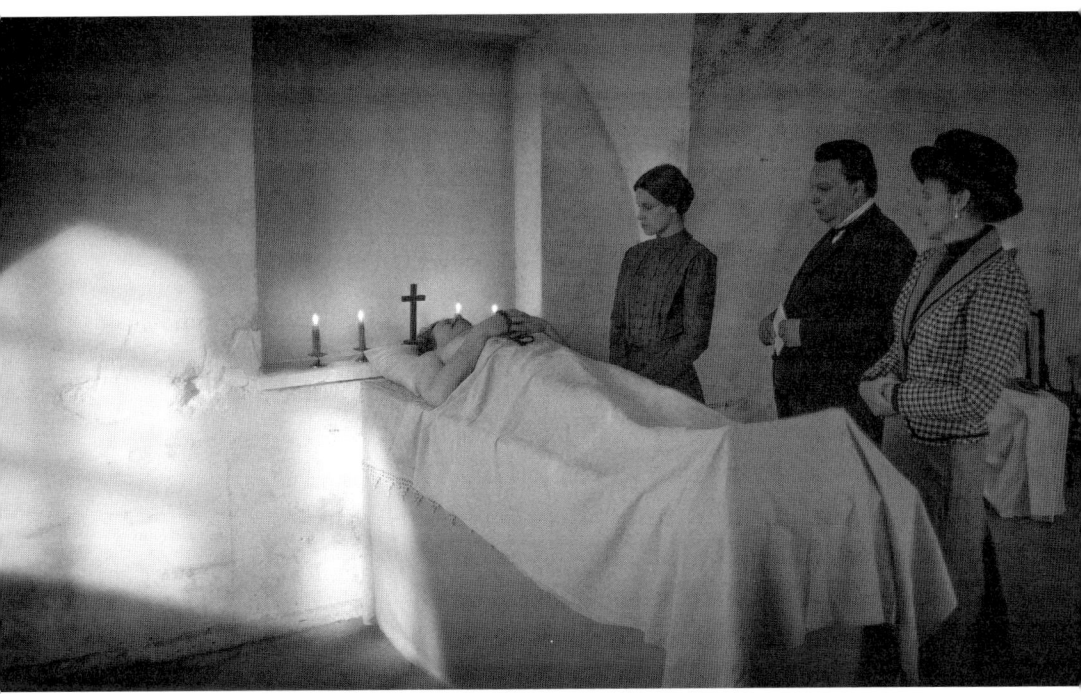

The deceased Čiurlionis lies in a hospital chapel, with Sofija (Marija Korenkaitė), her mother (Ramunė Skardžiūnaitė) and doctor (Edvard Keizik)

17

JUNE 2012

Up early after a very troubled sleep. Money worries and wondering whether I adequately covered Sofija (and Danūtė) and her mother being met by the doctor. It's my responsibility but I have to say I felt pressured not to shoot more than I did: Odd-Geir was clearly out of sorts and I think I lacked the courage to persuade him to shoot more.

It is back to the Dominican Monastery again, for the scene where Sofija sees her husband's corpse. Audrius has created a fine little chapel. We have a heater in the room because it's very, very, cold.

In the script I have Sofija pulling and punching Čiurlionis's body - being angry and sad at the same time. However, I've again also told Marija to do what she feels is right.

So, she sees Čiurlionis on the slab: tells Danūtė that "this is [her] Papa"; hands the baby to her mother; is handed a letter by the doctor (which is covered by a Čiurlionis voice-over); then she puts down the letter -which ends, "Zose, aren't we the lucky ones…"- and tears at his clothes: "am I so lucky now?" Then cries and puts her head on his chest.

*Mstislav Dobuzhinsky (Andrius Bialobžeskis)
and Čiurlionis discuss his paintings*

Odd-Geir is unconvinced, but I believe it to be a credible performance. Also, he doesn't know the voice-over that accompanies the scene.

Next up there are a couple of scenes with Andrius (Dobuzhinsky) and Rokas. Andrius is playing Dobuzhinsky very straight, very formal. It works.

We finish at 13:00 and the next scene isn't due to start until 18:00 (at the Writers' Building). The day has been poorly scheduled so I decide to go and do some GV's (clouds, forests, rooftops). Then I go outside and cannot see anything virtue of the relentless and ferocious rain. I call Artūras (production manager) and we try and find a way of starting in the Writers' Building at 16.00 - lunch until 14:00, some hanging around, then get into the building early. That's the plan and, surprisingly enough, Audrius (production designer) agrees that he can have it dressed by then.

The scene is Čiurlionis performing some piano music in front of a committee of cynics. It's wonderfully lit by candles (with Odd-Geir and Gena making it look utterly natural). The four men who constitute the committee -extras- need a lot of talking with and sadly I'm not as patient as I should be, but we get it done. I finish with a pull focus from a candle to Rokas's face, just in case I need it in the edit.

It is 18:00 we're finishing 4 hours early and the crew are ecstatic. It's raining heavily outside as I go to the office. I talk with Artūras about our big problems and small ones too - finance, and the logistics of next week's trip to the coast. There appear no easy solutions on the horizon.

I also again have toothache.

June 2nd

It's back to the Writers' Building for 4 scenes: Čiurlionis discussing some pictures with the Dobuzhinsky children; Čiurlionis and Dobuzhinsky discussing his work; Sofija and Mrs Dobuzhinsky discussing Čiurlionis; and, finally, Dobuzhinsky discussing Čiurlionis's paintings with a number of Russian art critics. In addition, the building has such a wonderful and grand staircase it would be foolish to ignore it. So I'm planning to do something on it.

The first scene is pretty straightforward in a beautifully dressed room, resplendent with furniture rented from Prague and stone fireplaces elaborately decorated.

Rokas and Andrius (Dobuzhinsky) do their thing; with Rokas saying some of the lines I've written that I quite like - "you're a mystic, Kastuk," to which Čiurlionis replies, "if I'm a mystic I'm a *Lithuanian* mystic." The scene is shot without too much difficulty, except that we have to put Andrius on a pillow so that his eye line matches that of Rokas.

Next up are the children, who first appeared at the Pushkin Museum. Rokas sits at the desk with them. They draw and then he discusses one of their drawings. It goes okay, although they don't react as much as I would like them to. I also shoot them playing with some wooden toys until I discover that the toys are modern: I'd assumed they were *period*. So, I shoot it again.

I do like the scene with Sofija and Mrs Dobuzhinsky (Agnė Sunklodaitė). We sit them on a sofa, and put a small table alongside (n.b., we're doing 4 scenes in the same room, but trying to make it appear as if they are quite different locations). They carry out their conversation flawlessly with no errors.

Before the next scene Odd-Geir tells me he's feeling unwell. I ask him if he wants to stop, but he says no. As if on cue Artūras comes to the set and reminds Odd-Geir that his bone scan will take place early on Monday. Then Artūras and I discuss the impact of the scan on the schedule. We decide that as the scan takes up to 4 hours we will have to have a Plan B. So, I tell Tomas (DIT) that I might need him on Monday as DOP for a couple of hours or so. He's happy to oblige: he's recently qualified as a DOP from Vilnius Academy and I've heard good things about him. He's also an extremely nice person, which helps enormously.

One of the scenes he might have to photograph is the re-shoot of the audience at the Philharmonic Hall (which we originally shot on March 8), because Inga was in the original schedule as Sofija.

Now we're shooting a scene with Dobuzhinsky and 3 art critics, who essentially dismiss Čiurlionis's work as unsophisticated and uninteresting. Indeed one of them says that his, "6 year old son could do better." I've not been looking forward to this scene, as it's not intrinsically sexy. However, I am really pleasantly surprised because one of the art critics possesses one of the best voices I've ever heard: Russian, deep, slow, powerful. I discover that this actor, Dmitrijus Denisiukas -one of 3 chosen by Jurga, the casting director, with me trusting her choices- is one of Lithuania's greatest voice-over artists, used regularly on commercials.

It all goes straightforwardly. Andrius (Dobuzhinsky) is very low key, which works well for both his character and the overall film, as many of the other members of the cast are extremely colourful.

Marija has gone to the hospital to visit her father who's just been admitted with pneumonia. We have to wait for her return before we can shoot the staircase scene. It works well -and, without question, the staircase is the star of the scene- except that Andrius calls Marija "Marija" and not Sofija.

We finish at 18.00 and not the scheduled 21.00, and so everyone is happy.

22:00

I am having an evening of incredible self-doubt. There are scenes, sequences, shot, missed shots, and performances that I'm concerned about. Hopefully, in the cutting room all will be revealed to be okay.

June 3rd

Wake up still worrying:

- I should have covered the shot when Sofija and her mother arrive to the sanatorium with a reverse and some cutaways. Odd-Geir persuaded me that we'd shot enough, but he was wrong. *My fault*.

- Rokas should have laughed when he uttered the "*Lithuanian* mystic" line.

More generally, on my day off, I ponder what I've learned so far:

- I must choreograph the moves better, especially to help the actors, DOP, focus puller.

- I must find more time to think about the shots and scenes *that lie ahead*.

- Not be bullied in anyway (especially by moody DOP's).

- Continue to try and be courteous to *everyone* concerned.

And in the future *always* ensure that the finance is fully in place before leaving home and not rely on half-baked promises or assumptions.

Tomorrow is a big day. I'm looking forward to it, so let's hope it isn't a bad omen.

Odd-Geir has decided *not* to take his cancer treatment here in Vilnius. He's contacted an old school friend -a retired brain surgeon- and has been persuaded that Oslo is where he should be. He says he'll finish the shoot first.

June 4th

Today is a day of big sequences, most notably when Čiurlionis and Sofija dance at a 'St. Petersburg Ball,' to be shot at the Vilnius Medal Gallery.

However, we begin at the Russian Drama Theatre where we are to re-shoot the one scene in which Inga appeared, namely, her audience reaction shots at the Philharmonic Hall. We can't use the seats at the Drama Theatre as they are different, but the structure of the theatre is the same. We make sure that all of the seats and armrests are covered by extras and their costumes.

Tomas (DIT) gets the old footage on his laptop and when he, Linus (focus puller) and Gediminas (camera assistant) see the footage they guffaw: "that was the old Sofija?" They are a little cruel, but the consensus (and hyperbole) is that Marija is "at least 100 times better."

I want to play some of *The Forest* so that Marija, the Dobuzhinskys' and the small group of extras can react more naturally to it. As usual, Marija is almost perfect.

*The re-shoot of Sofija (Marija Korenkaitė)
listening to The Forest (Miške)*

We move upstairs and prepare for two scenes, one where people congratulate Čiurlionis for his music and the other where Čiurlionis meets two young flirtatious Russian women. We shoot it in the corridor, which is quite sufficient: some Russian signs replace the no smoking signs. Also we had modern photographs on the wall replaced with some Russian art.

I am inexperienced with extras so it is hard work, but it gets done. Then we do the scene with two Russian girls, Natasha and Elena. Severija and Sasha, who I haven't seen since St. Petersburg, play them.

They stand by a door and we have a nice shot of them 'looking at Čiurlionis.' Then he passes by and they snare him into a conversation. This is all done smoothly, and we reverse the shot, etc. The scene ends with Dobuzhinsky looking on at his departure (with them) with an emotion of mild disappointment.

Lunch, and then the seduction scene - at the Medal Gallery. While we eat lunch Kestas visits the set and says that a) Artūras will have to sit down with the crew and explain our financial situation and b) that all future invoices will have to be in my and Rokas's names. It's a depressing start to the afternoon.

The 'seduction' scene will take place in a beautifully dressed room. Odd-Geir -who has a raging toothache and a temper to match- lights it imaginatively. However, he wants to start the shot with a tilt down from a chandelier but I don't like the shot, so we don't.

The two actresses take the scene seriously, but also with great humour. Rokas is a little nervous so I clear everyone, except the essential crew, out of the room. We rehearse the choreography, although I've also told the girls to play it as they wish.

All goes well, and they end up kissing him and blindfolding him with his tie. Then great laughter and a sense of relief. What Professor Landsbergis - self-appointed guardian of Čiurlionis and my *bête noire*- would think of this particular scene amuses me.

The rest of the day is spent with the St. Petersburg Ball. It is shot in a beautiful room, resplendent of those particular St. Petersburg *colours*, and with a magnificent gold French clock at one end of the room.

The quintet arrives and we put them in their place. They perform, the extras dance, I say hello to the Irish investor James Clarke's Russian wife, Marina, also an extra and a great dancer. They all swirl, the violins play, and on the monitor it looks quite wonderful.

We do a small scene where Dobuzhinsky meets Čiurlionis and offers to help sell his paintings. It goes well until the extra I ask to approach Dobuzhinsky and say "Slava" and take him away, *cannot stop talking*. He wants to add more and more, so in the end I show him exactly what to do.

I'm still having problems with the *axis*, crossing the line, etc.

Finally, we are ready to shoot a small scene where Čiurlionis reluctantly pulls Sofija onto the dance floor. However, by this time an appointment has been made at the dentist for Odd-Geir to have an extraction. So Tomas will shoot this final scene.

We rehearse, shoot it, and it looks great. Then, with 20 minutes left of the scheduled day, I ask Tomas if he could put the camera on his shoulder and follow Čiurlionis and Sofija around the dance floor. He does so and it is magnificent.

I get the call sheet for the following day, and it states at the top there's to be an important meeting for all of the 'Lithuanian crew' at 10:00 at the location.

I try and sleep but have a very restless night.

18

RAIN

June 5th

I awake to rain and, unfortunately, today is supposed to be a day we spend wholly *outside*. I meet Artūras and we drive to the location, some 30 minutes outside Vilnius. He is fully prepared to make the announcement to the meeting that a) there's no money, and b) that everyone will be paid by Rokas and me at the end of the shoot. How?

I press on.

The rain tumbles down and I become increasingly depressed. The first scene is due to be shot at 10:00 and at 12:00 we're still not ready. The meeting with Kestas has taken place, people have been told about the delay in payments, and happily most people are okay with it.

The scene is when the young Čiurlionis (17) watches a Chekhov play (*Uncle Vanya*) and turns to his father and says he's *doomed*.

In *Uncle Vanya* there's a character (Telegin) in the final scene, who strums his guitar. However, our guitarist is so bad that I have to replace him and re-shoot. The actor who plays the youthful Čiurlionis is a bit of a moaner and cries out, "I'm cold and wet."

So am I! My feet are wet, having been waiting for hours to start work in the pouring rain.

Čiurlionis's father (Vidas Petkevičius) has just returned from the Globe Theatre in London where he was performing in a Lithuanian version of *Hamlet*. We talk briefly about it and he remarks that he'd returned from "*London* Luton Airport."

The scene goes well and I particularly like the casting of Vanya and Sonya, two real Russian faces (chosen by casting director, Jurga) from the Russian Drama Theatre.

We shoot a few different angles and wait for Rokas and Marija as we are to repeat the scene with them - "I've been here before," says Čiurlionis as he watches the drama for the second time of his life. The first take sees Rokas overacting, looking like a madman. I ask him to simply look "sad," which he subsequently does and the scene is shot.

The rain has stopped.

We now have to prepare for 2 boating scenes: one in which Čiurlionis and Sofija kiss for the first time, and the other with Sofija and Danūtė in a boat talking about Danūtė's 'Papa.'

The first scene is accomplished quite easily, except for the occasion when Rokas hopelessly rows round and round in circles. Using the 300mm lens we achieve a wonderful close-up just as they pass us on the opposite side of the lake. Their kiss is innocent, which is good as their 'love' is supposed to be kind of 'pure.' It's a good job because I don't think Rokas likes kissing anyone but his wife.

Danūtė is 5 and the child cast to play her, Maja, is physically adequate but a little grumpy. I have to recruit her father to be close to her at all times.

The first sequence sees Maja with Sofija in the boat where she sees (the dead) Čiurlionis on the lakeside, and they leap out of the boat and greet him on the side of the lake. This scene is supposed to be achieved through a sketch of them in the boat, which then morphs into 'reality.'

We try it a few times -with, for example, the boat crashing into the jetty on one occasion- and then eventually, thankfully, it works.

I shoot two endings: one with Čiurlionis, Sofija and Danūtė, the other just with Sofija and Danūtė. I suspect I'll use the latter, especially because Rokas has been dressed in white -to match Sofija and Danūtė- and he looks uncannily like John Travolta from his *Saturday Night Fever* period.

Odd-Geir is in a particularly bad mood. He repeats his belief that I don't rehearse enough -true, but I have to be constantly cognisant of the time and the constraints of a demanding schedule- and in addition he has a new pain somewhere near his abdomen.

19

A HOBBIT TRAIN

June 6th

Today it is to the railway station at Anykščiai where we have to shoot a number of scenes. It's almost a two-hour drive and I know from Artūras's demeanour that he's stressed. After considerable prompting he tells me that although the shoot has been a happy experience for the cast and crew, including himself, the continuing financial anxieties make him feel ill.

When we arrive at the railway station and look at the carriages it is evident that they're not very well prepared: there's nothing special about the table covers or the curtains. However, we have the train booked *per hour* and I'm keen to get moving.

Eventually we stick down the tablecloths with double sided tape and then dress some of the tables with cups and saucers. We have 4 extras, a waitress, Rokas and a 'man.' This man and Rokas are to have a conversation about a sketch he's finishing -is it a child or the angel of death?- and it's an important scene. The train is narrow gauge and the carriages are, as we know, quite small. The actor cast for the 'man' is Valentinas Krulikovskis who looks too tall for what we refer to as the *Hobbit train*. But he turns out to be a fine actor for this small part.

We have a deal where we can stop and start the train to our heart's desire, which is what we do on a number of occasions. I start with the cutaways and the waitress delivering the drinks and cakes. All works well. Then we move on to the dialogue between Rokas and Valentinas. It is pretty straightforward and we do a reverse. Then we do 2 close-ups (two sizes) on the 'angel' sketch.

I then ask Odd-Geir to shoot the retreating railway tracks and then we're finished with the train. We now have to wait for it to turn around and head back to Anykščiai Station. I decide, on the return journey, to shoot one last scene in the train: from the window we'll shoot Marija looking forlorn at Rokas as he leaves for St. Petersburg. We set the shot up and call ahead to Artūras (at the station) to ensure that Marija is made-up and appropriately dressed.

We arrive, set the shot up, and it works according to plan.

We break for dinner and while some people eat, Artūras (production manager), Artūras (props-on-set) and Jonas (location scout) and I position two carriages alongside each other for the 'Vilnius Railway Station' scene. We will use lots of steam and smoke to hide the fact that this is in fact *not* Vilnius Railway Station.

It takes a long time to light -to ensure that the preceding scene on the train matches- and the sun is quickly fading. Rokas is also worried about his lines.

We do the scene and Rokas smiles too much, especially when Marija announces she's pregnant. I tell him and sadly he retreats to his prima donna mode. But, reluctantly, he agrees to tone it down.

The next take is better but then Giedrius (boom swinger) says the audio is poor. We shoot a much tighter version, stop the smoke machines, and Giedrius is happier. The sound engineer, Zigitas, is less happy, but that's his default mode.

We shoot Nikolaj standing in the smoke as if at the end of the platform. He's made the lengthy journey for a 20-second shot. The scene was in an early draft but I took it out: but Nikolaj pleaded for it to remain. So, I've shot it but I doubt if it will see the light of day.

The final scene of the day has Čiurlionis being taken home (to Druskininkai) by Sofija and his parents. We've re-painted the railway station sign and we do a nice shot of them approaching the entrance. We reverse, change lens and do a tighter shot that I particularly like.

End of the day. On the journey home we almost have a high-speed collision with an enormous elk. Apparently there are quite a few elks in Lithuanian forests, although greatly outnumbered by wild boar - which can be ferocious and are, at seemingly regular intervals, hunted by German tourists. However, the forests are really home to *mushrooms*, of all shapes and sizes.

June 7th

It's a 4-hour journey to the coast. In the car I can see already that Artūras is stressed. He repeats what he said the previous day: "this film has the best atmosphere on set, but the money situation is so stressful." What can I say?

We watch the countryside passing by, and also chat. We talk about marriage, parenting, the Soviet Union. He tells me about his mother's *dacha* and the system that -when it worked properly and according to the rules- rewarded workers with land on which they could spend their weekends and summers.

We wait and wait and *wait* for the actors. Eventually they arrive and we set up the first scene where the 17-year-old Čiurlionis wades into the sea, in a mesmerised state, and is rescued by his teacher, Prince Michal Ogiński. We only have two sets of identical clothes for them both so it *has* to work. It does, and we do two takes with different lenses. Saulius Balandis, who plays Oginski, has a fine head of hair, exudes aristocratic confidence and plays the piece perfectly. I subsequently learn that he is one of the few members of the cast who does popular television work.

The second (and last) scene of the day sees Čiurlionis and Sofija seated at the seashore, sharing a children's fairy tale. Rokas has an idea of telling the story with his hands, as in a puppet show. It works well and is his best performance so far.

At 23:20 we retreat to the hotel that turns out to be quite a surprise: a 4 star. I go for a drink with most of the crew to Palanga's main street, full of empty bars (as high season hasn't yet started). The first voices I hear are those of a rowdy and uncouth bunch of men from Birmingham.

We return to the hotel and go to the room where 'the girls' are: members of the make-up team, wardrobe department, Marija, et al. Champagne, wine, beer and brandy is enthusiastically drunk. All the conversation is in Lithuanian so I go to bed.

Sofija (Marija Korenkaitė) and Čiurlionis (Rokas Zubovas) on honeymoon, in Palanga

June 8th

Breakfast is at 09:30 and everyone is up and about despite drinking until 05:00. Artūras, however, is still asleep and so I go to the location and leave him at the hotel. The mixture of alcohol and stress means he needs his sleep!

We travel to the location for two scenes, connected, where Marija and Rokas enjoy their honeymoon by frolicking in the beachside forest, and then when Rokas runs into the sea. Rokas agrees to run into the water, *naked*, which we shoot discretely from his rear. The scene is carried out amidst great mirth and amusement. On the long lens it looks good. I do notice, however, how pale he is.

We are finished at Palanga by 13:00, have a seemingly endless lunch (because of the numbers of us that need to be served), and return to Vilnius for one last scene.

I've added a new scene involving Sofija and Rostov, in order to hopefully show a different side to him as, so far, all he's done is intimidate everyone he encounters and kill Catholics. So, I have Sofija finding him in a library reading Turgenev's *Fathers and Children* (translated outside of Russia as *Fathers and Sons*). The scene plays out as a kind of flirtatious game of 'who knows most about Russian literature?' The aim of the scene is to show the sophisticated and marginally humorous side to Rostov.

We shoot at one of the government's book storage centres in Vilnius. Marija and Nick play the scene well, which is good considering Marija's slight problem with Russian.

We finish early, and I watch Russia beat the Czech Republic in the European football championship.

20

TRAKU VOKE

Up early. Feel slightly 'low in mood.' For the rest of the shoot we are based at a place called Traku Voke -a stately home in disrepair in a small village also called *Traku Voke*. We have a number of sets within this location - Sofija's parents' house; Čiurlionis's Vilnius and St. Petersburg apartments; and, finally, a doctor's consulting room.

We are shooting two important scenes today: one where Sofija meets Čiurlionis and he shows her his painting *Friendship*, which shows a woman holding a sphere - "look you appeared in my dreams even before we met"- and another scene where he tells Sofija he's leaving for St. Petersburg (after being threatened by Rostov).

Čiurlionis's (Vilnius) apartment is incredibly small although it does have a removable fake wall.

The first scene goes reasonably well, although I have to gently encourage Rokas to smile less. Despite my gentle encouragement he slinks off in a huff. I send Marija off after him and he subsequently returns after a lengthy 30 minutes.

They play the scene well.

We then have 2 short scenes with the baby (a boy who is playing a girl). Marija is not at all used to babies and it shows, but we struggle through to the end. However, in the end, we use the doll (which is incredibly ugly) for the close ups of Marija and also the cutaways. We put a bonnet on the doll and it works adequately.

We have a late lunch (16:00) and prepare for the main scene. Rokas is again anxious and tetchy, unsurprisingly perhaps given that he's a musician and not an actor.

We shoot the scenes in numerous, separate parts, and then slowly move towards the main action where Čiurlionis smashes a bottle of vodka against the wall.

I tell Rokas that he has to act. *Really* act. This is when he has to change from the gentle sensitive soul he's so far managed to project, to the seemingly heartless bastard. He does it incredibly well. His voice changes and he smashes the bottle with real venom.

We need to do it 3 times but only have 2 bottles. So Artūras (props-on-set) and I walk to the local shop. We buy a similar bottle, and the guy who sells it to me tells me to, "enjoy it." I tell him we're not going to drink it, but simply break the bottle. He looks at me with a mixture of disgust and puzzlement.

We return to the set and Artūras changes the label on the bottle, and we re-shoot the scene. However, for some strange reason the bottle doesn't break. I neither laugh nor cry, just re-shoot and this time there's broken glass everywhere. The scene has emotionally drained both of them.

We wrap and I arrange to meet Rokas later to watch football. It's Germany versus Portugal, is tedious and made worse by the numerous fat and noisy English drinkers in the bar.

June 10th

Have a quiet day, cleaning the apartment and doing some packing. I also go to a café, get online and book a ticket for Thursday morning to the lovely London Luton Airport.

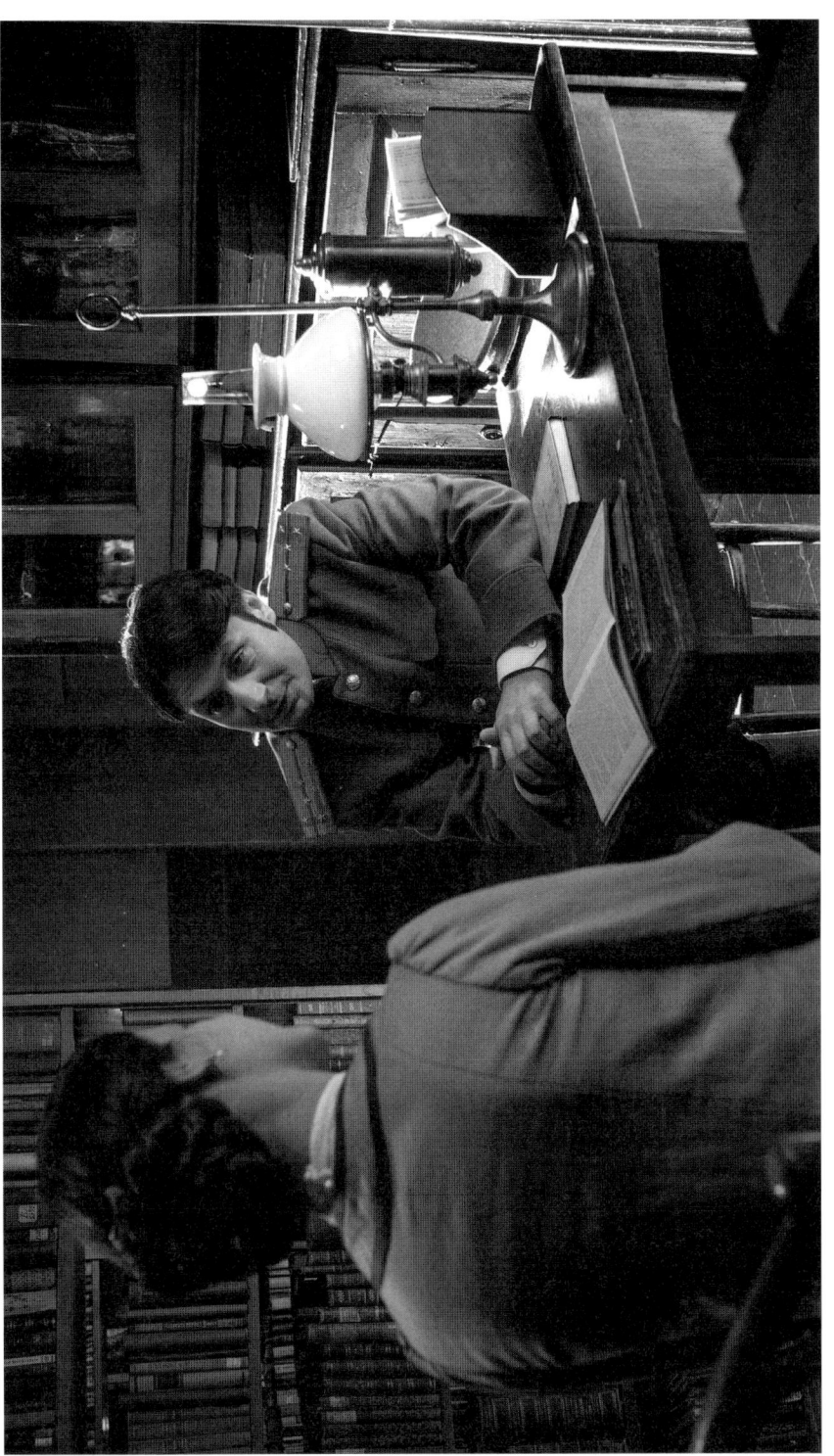
Sofija (Marija Korenkaitė) and Captain Rostov (Nikolaj Antonov) discuss Russian literature

I send numerous emails including one about the need to re-shoot one aspect of yesterday's shoot. I realise that I need to see Rokas actually throw the bottle.

I take the short walk to Mano Guru for some food and am appalled by the music, which is some kind of American rap. You could perceive it as another example of a more or less subtle imperialism. Indeed, I also read today that over one third of the Lithuanian's governmental budget is from the EU. So much for Lithuanian *independence*.

June 11th

Up early today and off to Traku Voke again, with more important scenes to shoot.

I can tell at first sight that Rokas is in one of his moods, so I anticipate some prima-donnish behaviour.

Two scenes are quickly shot - with Čiurlionis looking depressed, sitting by a wall and then staring into a mirror, and then lighting a fire in his St. Petersburg apartment while Sofija looks on. We actually light a fire and create chaos with uncontrollable smoke.

There's also a big scene with Čiurlionis returning home after his late night encounter with the two Russian women, and with Sofija subsequently leaving him after a lengthy and pained conversation.

We need to shoot this many, *many*, times because Rokas consistently gets a line wrong. I say, "look, the camera's on your back, so write down the line and read from it - we won't see the sheet of paper." He refuses. Eventually we somehow complete the scene.

Next up, in Čiurlionis's Vilnius apartment, Sofija asks him to play the piano. He does so, gently performing *Opus II*. Then he tells her he must go to St. Petersburg to try and find work. This goes without a hitch.

We re-shoot the vodka bottle-smashing incident.

Marija (Sofija) next gives birth. She is quite incredible, and most of us are alarmed at the sound of her screams. We bring in the real baby at the last moment. It's all done tastefully with no blood or anything gory like that.

Finally, there's a scene with Sofija and her mother where they talk about both Nikolaj and Čiurlionis. We shoot it in the conservatory (full of plants) and it works well, except that the art department have used some 1960's plant pots in some places. So we spend quite a while fixing the furniture.

I am tired, demob happy, and go to watch France play England in a Vilnius bar.

June 12th

The last but one day of shooting and my day begins with worries about finances - I have to find money in a few weeks' time to pay people. How on earth am I going to do that? I certainly have given up on Kestas et al. helping as previously agreed.

Anyhow, off again to Traku Voke.

The first scene involves Sofija and her father and it precedes the scene we shot last thing yesterday with Sofija and her mother, which makes me realise that I've made a mistake not including Sofija's mother in the scene with her husband. Actually, Jelena pointed out the error. Luckily Ramunė (Sofija's mother) is already scheduled to appear today so we change her call time and start only one hour late. She's fine about it.

The scene works well, and Mr Kymantas shows his disapproval of his daughter's future husband very effectively.

Next up is Rostov's attempt to win the approval of Sofija's parents. This is all done very well, especially after I encourage Nikolaj (Rostov) to act less formally than usual.

We shoot both of these scenes with extensive coverage. This takes time and so we lunch at 14:00.

After lunch Rostov threatens Čiurlionis in the latter's apartment. He does this so effectively and with such great surprise and suddenness that everyone is shocked, and Rokas's throat is sore.

Indeed we have to get Nikolaj to repeat his grabbing of Rokas's throat a few times. He also knocks over an easel quite unexpectedly and dramatically.

I ordered 2 sketches for a particular scene (the boat on the lake) but only 1 arrived: Audrius says only one freeze frame was sent, while Tomas (DIT) says he sent two. I'm irritated although it isn't the end of the world.

Finally, we do two scenes with Rokas -at his final St. Petersburg apartment- where he is lying on the floor, depressed. One of these is day the other is night, both with Rokas half-naked. Both are beautifully lit.

Home time.

A 'wrap party' has been arranged for tomorrow but I have to pay for it. The financial misery never ends.

Tonight, I am going to watch Russia play Poland at football. It's dreary, except for a fabulous goal from the Polish captain, Jakub Blaszczykowski.

21

TO 'LONDON' LUTON AIRPORT

June 13th

The final day of shooting. Truth told, I am relieved. I have found it difficult coping with all the different languages -Russian, Lithuanian and Polish- in addition to sharing an apartment with a Norwegian DOP suffering prostate cancer.

Somewhat, miraculously, the sketch for the scene on the lake arrives and I quickly stick it on the wall and shoot it.

The first scene is the post-funeral dinner where Sofija delivers a short speech. She's re-arranged what I've written which is fine by me. I spend over an hour on reaction shots and it pays dividends when Čiurlionis's mother sheds real tears. I have to chastise 'Juzefa' and remind her that her beloved 'brother' has just died.

I feel tetchy and it shows.

There are a couple of short scenes involving Rokas, in different states of despair, and then the main action follows, a family Christmas dinner.

We have a young boy -8 or 9- singing a Lithuanian 'Christmas song.' This turns out to be *Silent Night* in the Lithuanian language. He does this beautifully and we compose a shot from a set of candles and pan to his face.

Just afterwards the second AD, Ieva, approached me (tentatively) and said that the Lithuanian version of *Silent Night* was not actually written at the correct time and was, in fact, a post-1908 interpretation. Great. Not what I wanted to hear.

While I was thinking what to do about the problem, the first AD, Pius, said he'd googled the interpretation and it was in fact pre-1908! While the two AD's further discussed the matter I asked the boy's mother if he could sing anything else. "No."

I decide to live with *Silent Night*.

I do some close ups on beetroot, fish and various pickles. Then the lovely Ramunė -Sofija's mother- sings a little song with the boy on her lap and it looks very familial and natural.

The scene is a success. There's just one little scene to shoot where Sofija and her mother breakaway from the dinner and talk about Konstantinas being alone in St. Petersburg. Odd-Geir lights it beautifully and it is shot without any great difficulties.

20:00

The wrap party was a noisy affair, and many of the crew looked technically speaking 'blind drunk,' but various crew and cast members showed great tenderness towards me. There are surprises, especially on the dance floor where Gena -burly, and fearsome looking, albeit with a sweet smile- hugs me.

June 14th

At 02:00 I slip away, but people see me, applaud and embrace me. I now feel very sad to be leaving.

At 05:00, I am on the flight back to London Luton Airport.

AFTERWORD

The initial idea for this diary was to write about the film's *production*, rather than the post-production period (editing, grading, mixing, etc.) or completion of the project, yet I feel that I should say *something* about *what happened next*.

Before I do so I would like to return to the main players in the project - *Odd-Geir*, *Kestas* and *Rokas*. Although the production was facilitated by a large team of cast and crew (not to forget *investors*), these three people were central to the project and my day-to-day life.

Odd-Geir taught me a lot, especially the fact that there is actually nothing quite as valuable as *experience*, and of course he himself possessed a lifetime's worth of shooting feature films and television dramas. Odd-Geir appeared unfazed by any request I made of him, offered solutions to any problems that emerged and, importantly, was full of his own ideas and suggestions. I could list innumerable shots he set up and executed, but perhaps I should just recall his wonderful shooting at Palanga and the Baltic Sea with, for example: Čiurlionis and Sofija running alongside the beach; sharing the fairy tale of the 'sun, the moon and Perkūnas' by the seashore (with Odd-Geir shooting day-for-night); and, finally, the wonderfully evocative scene where Prince Ogiński walks along the beach and talks with the young Čiurlionis about the mythical origins of *amber*. However, all was not plain sailing: for example, we shared the same Vilnius apartment; we worked day and night together; we were both unpaid and under pressure and, just to cap it all, Odd-Geir worked with the cloud of a negative medical diagnosis hanging over him. *More specifically, we were both imperfect human beings.*

    I find confrontation difficult and, as a result, can often shy away from decision-making or conflict resolution: conversely, Odd-Geir has no difficulties with expressing his opinions or feelings! Indeed, he would regularly and wryly remark on his reputation as being 'bad tempered.'

    I frustrated him by my over-eagerness to *get on with things*, rather than taking more time, rehearsing more and fully choreographing sequences, especially the more complex ones. Through his (at times) bad tempered interventions *I learned a lot* (although no one but me appears to fully understand the fact that *the restrictions and constraints of time* is the relentless enemy of any production).

    Kestas and I repeatedly 'fell out.' However, he also allowed the production to use his (and Artbox's) resourceful and good-humoured casting director; the casting and make-up suites; office space, and some general support, so his contribution to the overall effort was evident. Both of us were frustrated about the financial aspects of the production, and both of us suffered constantly at the litany of broken promises delivered straight-faced by numerous entrepreneurs and sponsors. The fact is that some relationships are easier to sustain than others.

    Central to *Letters to Sofija* was the acting, piano playing, the organisation of the recording of Čiurlionis's orchestral music, and the general enthusiasm of *Rokas*. His dedication to the project was second-to-none: for example, he spent over 4 months eating only raw food in an attempt to lose a considerable amount of weight. More importantly, he was widely respected -by the members of the Lithuanian Philharmonic Orchestra, other members of the cast and crew, local politicians and fixers- and possessed the ability to make people do things they might otherwise have resisted. He'd never before professionally acted, and had only engaged in the art while at the Music Academy. But he threw himself into the leading role, excelled in it and, for the most time, carried out the work with good grace.

However, at times, the pressure told and he behaved less-than-perfectly, especially to me. I'd perfectly understand the situation he was in, but wouldn't appreciate his behaviour and probably didn't handle such situations appropriately. Rokas also strenuously worked with me on all aspects of fund raising, was always a brilliant ambassador -when meeting politicians and the business community- and put his spirit into the role and the film.

Rokas probably knows more about Čiurlionis, his great-grandfather, than any other living person. For example, listen to and read the accompanying literature, of his *M K Čiurlionis: Compositions for Piano* (2011), for proof of his extensive knowledge and *love* of this most-neglected artist. It was therefore unsurprising that he didn't approve of everything I did, both in the production process and also with the post-production creation of the *music* score.

Hopefully our relationship will survive.

As mentioned earlier, *the post-production of the film* was to take place at Prime Focus in London (and, possibly, India or the USA). This had been arranged, somewhat informally and casually, with the company's COO, Anshul Doshi, and was facilitated by my friendship with one of their consultants, Michael Elson. And, so it began.

However, I was still saddled with the need to raise some finance to pay outstanding invoices, given that I was not receiving any help from my Lithuanian colleagues. Happily this problem was speedily solved through the intervention of my new business partner and colleague who, through personal sacrifices and his own money, saved the day.

So, on to the edit.

It would be quite easy to contribute another 40,000 words on the editing process itself, but in the absence of detailed notes much of this would be highly anecdotal and perhaps inaccurate. But, it is worth discussing the post-production process in some degree of detail, especially as the purpose of this short book is to assist others and help them avoid some of the many mistakes I've made and situations I've created that have proved less than helpful.

Lesson number one: never accept an offer of a *free* post-production deal without understanding precisely what this might actually entail. In my mind I'd imagined that I would return to the UK with the material -hard drives, with 2 terabytes worth of material - and immediately get down to editing. In fact, there was a lengthy initial delay to get the material into sync because I was way down the company's list of priorities. What followed was a series of delays and difficulties *all created* by the fact that various line managers didn't fully understand what I had been offered by the COO of the company and because 'free jobs' are never given the equal status of fully-paid jobs - perhaps understandably so, but frustrating nonetheless.

After the delay of getting the material into sync, we -my long-time friend and colleague, Laurie Yule- began the process of editing.

An aside: Laurie and I worked together on a series for the Discovery Health Channel that focussed on the psychological and physical effects of losing a limb. In particular, the series was intended to highlight the differences between different kinds of injuries and limb loss, and the differences between various kinds of prosthetics (some basic, others high tech). This 4 part series was tentatively titled, *Life and Limb*. Laurie worked as an assistant cameraman on the project and I directed and produced the series. In the USA we met a multitude of heroic individuals, from war veterans to diabetic amputees, from the old and grizzled to small vulnerable wide-eyed children. Despite the somewhat depressing and painful subject matter, the majority of the actual work was enjoyable: from the reminiscences of individuals, like the diabetic man from New York who claimed that he partially awoke from anaesthesia to find the surgeon at work removing his leg while listening to Led Zeppelin's *Whole Lotta Love*, to a Baltimore man who claimed (supported by his physician) that he could feel pleasure and pain in his absent limb (removed five years previously), and from the company of an American crew – a motley group of fellow neurotic individuals, including a driver who refused to drive us unless we were prepared to endure the music of Van Halen at monstrous decibels. However, from a 'professional' point of view, the series stays in my memory because of something one of the Discovery executives 'shared' with me.

I'd had the privilege of meeting a small 9-year-old boy who, because of some accident of birth, had knees that joined his ankles. This absence of lower legs had led to numerous operations and, ultimately, sophisticated and effective prosthetics. Despite theses adverse life events he was a cheery chap and a reasonably good ice hockey player. I filmed an interview with him and his parents and, in addition, shot some general scenes. I mentioned this to the Discovery executive, who immediately fantasised a scene: 'Mom opens bedroom curtains. We see a small boy in bed. Voice over: "But this is no ordinary boy: Tommy has no legs."'

Diplomatically I told him that I had a different idea for the scene, namely focussing on the boy's own careful and insightful reflections on his disability and the manner in which he has dealt with it - after all, I reasoned, his insight was quite remarkable for a 9-year-old. The executive spat bile: "Don't you know *anything* about this business! Write a commentary and treat your audience *as if* they are children, make it simple and stupid. Pretend your audience has the intellectual level of a 7-year-old."

This incident reminded me of an exchange I had a few years earlier with an executive at Anglia Television who, tired of yet another 'intellectual programme idea' I'd submitted, sighed: "Bob, the trouble with you is that you simply don't understand the *great unwashed*. They are thick bastards who work all day and want their tiny brain cells tickled and titillated in the evenings, not have them stimulated."

These two men were part of the reason I've always yearned to leave television with its relentless dive down into anti-intellectualism. I've never felt at ease with the oft-quoted mantra, 'give people what they want.' I've always felt happier with the idea that we could actually give people what they *need*, rather than *want*. It might sound élitist but, sadly, the truth is that if we actually asked quite a number of people what they wanted personally to see on television they might well say 'public executions,' a close up of Saddam Hussein's hanging, lengthy scenes of Colonel Gaddafi's bloodied body being dragged through the streets of Sirte, fawning documentaries on the Queen and other Royals, various forms of pornography, and so on.

So, Laurie and I began to edit *Letters to Sofija*. The first thing we noticed was that we'd been put in a room that was both small and excruciatingly hot: top of the building and away from the suites that housed paid work. Next thing we noticed was the small and foggy monitor, on which our footage could barely be seen. After a number of telephone calls we were able to have the monitor replaced, at our expense, and another one delivered in its place. This one wasn't much better.

I constantly began to tell myself, "however difficult this edit becomes, remember - it's free, or at least, should I say, so far no one has talked with me about what Prime Focus wants in return for giving me the opportunity to edit at their facilities."

After three weeks of editing -on a small monitor, with the sun shining aggressively through the window, and with both Laurie and I feeling like interlopers- it became evident that the middle management would like us to *fuck off*, vacate the editing suite and allow some commercial clients in.

One memorable day it became clear that it would be our last day in the offline.

However, after numerous emails and begging phone calls, we were granted a few more days in two different suites - one in another building the company owned, and on an even higher floor.

A final *final* day arrived and we had about 4 hours to view our 2-hour film and make any changes we thought were required. Duh!

Mermaids.

My good friend Michael Elson had introduced me to a student team at the University of Kent who very keen to create (through CGI) my mermaids, as part of their MSc and as a potential calling card for future employment. They offered up the opportunity for me to revert to my original dream, namely that Rokas (Čiurlionis) would voice-over images of the myth and story of Kastytis (the fisherman) and Jūratė (Queen of the mermaids), which would be created through CGI.

The potential for a magnificent set of scenes was evident: a fisherman kissed and then pulled underwater by a smiling mermaid; she would then lead him by the hand to her Amber Palace, reached through a mazy trip through the deep sea; he would meet a Choir of Mermaids; he would almost drown; and, ultimately, their illicit romance would be destroyed by Perkūnas, God of Thunder, who would destroy the Palace, the Choir of Mermaids and send the heartbroken Kastytis back to land.

The students seemed very enthusiastic, but over a short few weeks some clearly appeared to have a little more talent or motivation than the others: some of the images were wonderful, like the central one of Jūratė, who had been created *as if* she was an underwater beauty wearing a costume designed by Gustav Klimt. Other images were poor, unfinished and utterly inadequate.

On our final *final* day we were faced with a decision: either to ditch *all* the CGI images or try and find a way in which to use the few good ones. In the end I decided to start the film describing the Kastytis and Jūratė myth *in text* underneath three sets of CGI. It was a disappointing end to a seemingly possible dream, but at least *some* of the work was salvaged. Most disappointing was the fact that all of the numerous sections of voice over that Rokas had recorded -with his quite beautiful and seductive voice- would now be totally redundant, unused and forever forgotten.

'It can be fixed in post'…

For much of the time while actually shooting, we were highly cognisant of the fact that *Sofija* was a period film and therefore we had to be acutely aware so as to avoid any post-1908 items, costumes, fixtures or fittings. At times this had proved to be a task of nightmarish proportions: for example, in St. Petersburg, every 18th and 19th building appeared to be adorned with pieces of MacDonald's or other corporate advertising. I may be perhaps exaggerating a little, but you get the point.

Odd-Geir's response to these endless concerns was, at times, to utter the oft-heard mantra: "don't worry, it can be fixed in post." Now, of course, much *can* be achieved in post but *this costs money, takes time*, and perhaps most importantly, isn't *always* successful.

As our edit progressed we did indeed discover that we had failed to avoid some unwanted items. For example, in one scene where Sofija and Čiurlionis meet outside the office of *Viltis*, her place of work, a large modern padlock is clearly in shot. We all failed to see this - neither Jelena (continuity), Odd-Geir (DOP), nor I, spotted it. This item was merely one of *many* - for example, a small boat on the Baltic Sea, satellite dishes and CCTV cameras on buildings in both Vilnius and St. Petersburg, the newspaper editor's hearing aid clearly in shot (three times) at Čiurlionis and Sofija's wedding reception, an *Oxfam* wristband on one of the extras operating the printer at *Viltis*, modern lights in shot, and so on.

These unwanted items would have to be dealt with -if we were allowed the time and cost involved- in either the online editing process or the grade (when the colour is returned to the pictures and tweaked).

However, our online experience was a deeply unhappy one. In addition to the removal of a few unwanted items, it involved the creation and placement of over 2000 subtitles - English subtitles on the international version of the film, and Lithuanian subtitles over the Russian and Polish dialogue for the Lithuanian version.

Our online editor had never created as many subtitles and, I suspect, he found it a tedious activity. He certainly behaved as if he found the work not to his liking.

Prior to this process Laurie and I had to check the accuracy of the dialogue we'd already chosen and edited: we had to answer the question - had we correctly put together the Lithuanian, Russian and Polish dialogues, or had we missed sentences or words? We invited a friend from Lithuania to come over for a few days and watch the rough cut and check the dialogue. Luckily, and miraculously, we'd made very few mistakes, and they were easily fixed. But placing the subtitles in exactly the right place was trickier and took a long time.

The online editor repeatedly and regularly made us aware that we were being 'fitted in' to his schedule in between his 'real work,' in other words: clients who he knew were paying the full or slightly reduced rates. It got to the stage where we were reluctant to ask the simplest of requests: for example, "could you try and find a better font for that caption, please?" In the end the relationship ended in tears with him referring to me as a 'serpent' -truly- and Laurie and I disgusted at his lack of professionalism.

We discussed this perceived lack of professionalism with his line manager, someone quite important in the grand scheme of things, and she agreed that despite our "freeloader status" the editor should have treated us as just like any other client. Sadly, I suspect he can't help himself and that this *is* how he treats *all* his clients.

Next up was the *grade* which was, happily, a much more agreeable experience. We shared the delightful company of one of Prime Focus's senior colourists who was both interested in the project, utterly professional and simply nice to be with. We spent quite a bit of time removing unwanted items -the *Oxfam* bracelet springs to mind- but most of all we simply enhanced colours and corrected some mistakes. Only one scene -when Čiurlionis walks at night through the rainy forest- required extensive and lengthy work. It appeared too 'surreal' and we therefore adjusted colours so that it looked more 'realistic.' While in the grade we additionally straightened a few walls, brought out detail in curtains and also added some twinkling stars.

The *sound mix* wasn't as enjoyable as we'd hoped or anticipated. To begin with, the schedule was uncertain and constantly changed: we were due to start on the Monday, then it was the Wednesday, then it would be the following week, and so on. When we *did* eventually get inside the sound studio we were told in no uncertain terms that we had the suite and the editor for a few days and then that was "it."

I am a huge fan of audio and get easily annoyed at its general underestimation. It constitutes *at least* 50 per cent of any film, yet is often disregarded in terms of its importance. For instance, the camera department always appear to ignore the contribution of audio until a boom is in shot, then they quickly realise that there are two main production departments at work.

The audio department had cleaned up the dialogue and produced some effects, like the sound of horse-drawn carriages passing by outside the various interiors. It was, at best, workmanlike. However, given the restrictions on our time -"you have so many days of mixing then you can review what we've done, make quick changes, then go"- the mix never fully satisfied either Laurie or I. There was insufficient time for either reflection or for the finessing of the material. All in all it was a great disappointment.

A DCP -digital cinema package (a hard disk)- was eventually created, but not without numerous difficulties and a lengthy and unnecessary wait, and then a preview was arranged for October 16th at the Moving Picture Company, partly arranged by the Lithuanian Embassy in London. This would be the first time we'd seen the film on a cinema screen with a surround sound system.

I spent some time with the projectionist, because we'd put subtitles on the black spacing *below* the picture -why would you spoil the images by putting subtitles on top of them?- and s/he needed to know that fact.

The evening went well, although I noticed a couple of guests -mainly, although not exclusively, Lithuanian- laughing at an 'inappropriate place.' At the end of the screening, the Lithuanian Ambassador told me that I'd captured the rural spirit of Lithuania and that he'd certainly liked the film; various friends and family said they enjoyed it, and most of them commented on the power and grace of Marija's performance, while my wife commented on the beauty of Rokas's voice; and afterwards, over a few drinks, many people said they were emotionally moved by the film and enjoyed seeing Čiurlionis as a 'flesh and blood character.'

At the screening, Laurie and I noticed at least two audio problems, slight but noticeable: one was the quiet but distinct sound of a lamp buzzing, the other one was a case of discernible camera noise. As for pictures and performances, I knew immediately that there were a number of scenes I would like to change. But it was now invariably too late.

A few weeks later I then travelled to Vilnius to show the completed film to 'cast and crew.' So, on a cold and drizzly November evening I sat next to Marija and Valentinas, one of the crew's drivers, who irritated me by texting while the film was showing. Marija sat still.

The general consensus was that the film was 'good,' although no one except Rokas's wife, Sonata, was wildly enthusiastic. Sonata said I'd created a "fine piece of art" and that pleased me. But I went to bed paranoid.

The next day I met Kestas who said -with far too much enthusiasm for my liking (and fragile ego)- that the film would "never get distributed in Lithuania," that there was too much overacting, especially by Marija, that "Rokas mumbled his words," and many more negative comments. I left his office deeply upset and realised, once again, that perhaps my skin was insufficiently thin for this type of endeavour.

I met with Rokas; shared some coffee, and he assured me that whatever anyone else said, the film had been well received and that I should ignore Kestas. He *did*, however, ask whether he could play with the soundtrack and I had to firmly say "no." I understood entirely his desire to change the music, as he felt himself to be somewhat of a guardian of his great-grandfather's work, but I felt he never understood the need to sync the pictures with the music.

This second cinema viewing of the film made me realise that before I could try and get a distributor interested I had to make some changes, some minor, others not so. *For example*: there were some incorrect accents on a number of actors' names in the opening titles; in the scene where Čiurlionis shows Sofija his painting *Friendship*, the cut appeared to make the painting *jump*; in the library scene, where Captain Rostov tries to impress Sofija with his knowledge of Russian literature, it appeared too long and I wondered whether I should cut out some of the middle dialogue; we cut the scene at the jeweller's shop too soon, and the cut needed extending; I realised that we should start the scene with Rostov and Sofija at *Viltis* with a shot of Rostov *already seated*, rather than the slower build up to their hostile conversation; the train carriage scene where Čiurlionis discusses a sketch of his with another passenger, simply didn't seem to work; should I abandon the second *Uncle Vanya* scene, not because of any inherent problem, but simply to reduce the overall length of the film?; should I reduce the length of the scene where Čiurlionis plays the piano in the sanatorium, because it seemed to drag a little?; should I reduce the length of Dobuzhinsky saying goodbye to Čiurlionis at the sanatorium?; should I omit the exterior of the *Viltis* office? I'd never been happy with it, because of the distance from which it was shot; I definitely had to omit the art gallery scene before the café conversation and replace it with a close up of a painting; I had to check two stutters that Rokas appears to make; it was essential to re-grade the Vilnius church shots, as they appear *too white*; the font on the final card on the Lithuanian version needed changing, as it was too large and somewhat inappropriate, unsubtle;

the font on on the English subtitles needed to be changed, replaced with something more subtle; and for the sake of continuity I needed to change a shot when Čiurlionis and Sofija first arrive at St. Petersburg station - one minute she is on the left of him, the next she is on the right. There is the intervening element of train smoke and steam, but although it seemed okay in the edit, it doesn't now.

I return to Prime Focus, talk and argue, and, happily, they decide it is possible for me to have a little more time in various suites. Everyone tries to appear helpful, but their heart is not in it. Eventually, a couple of weeks later, another DCP is produced.

Next up is a visit to Chicago to show the film to Marty Rubin, the curator of the European Union Film Festival, held annually at the well-known Gene Siskel Film Center. *Letters to Sofija* will be viewed and he -in association with the Lithuanian Embassy's cultural attaché in Chicago, and a few other locals- will decide whether the film should represent Lithuania.

The flight to Chicago takes longer than I expected, the films on the plane are poor, but I really like the city. I am staying at a mid-range hotel and spend the first night watching *Crossfire Hurricane* on television, the documentary about the Rolling Stones. It's quite predictable, but some of the footage of the Stones in their pomp is magnificent.

I take the DCP to the cinema and then await the handful of people who will judge the film. There are about six or so people, some women and some men.

I watch the film again and of course find even more mistakes and things that, had I the opportunity, would do differently. Happily, no one else appears to notice the mistakes, unless of course they are being diplomatic. In particular, I notice a slight hum in the scene where the doctor tells Sofija that her beloved husband has unexpectedly died.

The reaction of the group confirms what I have already perceived elsewhere: *that women prefer the film to men*. On every showing of the film many women cry near the end of the film, especially when Sofija is told of Čiurlionis's death and when she shows her baby daughter, Danutė, his corpse, lying on a slab in a small hospital chapel. Then when at the post-funeral dinner she make a short speech and says that he will always live on in her heart.

After the viewing I am invited to dinner by the Lithuanian Embassy staff. We walk a few hundred metres to a large, noisy, 'fish and steak' house. Eyebrows are raised when I announce my vegetarian status, but the evening progresses amiably, *until* I mention my next project, which is about a Lithuanian Holocaust survivor - against the backdrop of the extensive Lithuanian collaboration with the Nazis.

The mood changes and I am soon lectured on the so-called *double genocide thesis*. This is the idea proposed and perpetuated by the current Lithuanian government that asserts that we should give equal status to the crimes committed against Lithuanians by Stalin, to those crimes committed against the Jews in the Lithuania of 1939-1944. Of course these are quite different types of crime and circumstances, but the Lithuanian government is keen to *rewrite history*, especially where it concerns the collaboration of its government and many volunteers in the murders of Jews committed by the Nazis.

I leave the restaurant soon afterwards and go to bed thinking that there is now no chance of *Sofija* being selected.

I spend a couple of extra days in Chicago -in order to comply with the cheap air fare- and enjoy wandering around a few museums, bookshops and parks. Am fascinated and impressed by the *L ('elevated') train*, rumbling over my head as I endlessly walk the streets. For me, the only downside to Chicago is the high number of homeless black men I encounter, many claiming an army or forces background, all cold, all without money.

When I eventually arrive back home I hear that the film has indeed been chosen to represent the nation at the EU Festival!

In early 2013 *Letters to Sofija* (with English *and* Lithuanian subtitles) was shown three times at *Kino Pavasaris*, Lithuania's premier film festival, to an apparently positive reception by the large audiences. One showing was at a Vilnius multiplex, one screening was in Kaunas, and finally there was a screening at a Vilnius arthouse cinema. And despite being told that the film would not be distributed in Lithuania (and therefore elsewhere in the Baltics), a deal was made in March 2013 with ACME, the Baltics' largest distributor, for the film to be distributed from the autumn of 2013. We still await an international deal, but there are positive signs of interest.

Despite being now preoccupied with a new film, a future film and endless other projects, *Sofija* remains a work-in-process. For example, the soundtrack is currently being completed and will be released in the autumn of 2013 and, as intimated, work continues for a distribution deal to be signed so that audiences throughout the world can see the film.

My initial and primary aim in making the film was to *try* and tell the world about an undiscovered artist who possessed great talent, a unique vision and whose life was short and troubled. An artist who created paintings and music while struggling with a precarious mental state, a man who loved his country and also a woman whose love he had so little time to enjoy.

I think I have achieved the aim of telling the world about Mikalojus Konstantinas Čiurlionis.

March 2013